The New American-ism

and other
speeches
and

essays

by

Robert
Welch

foreword by

Robert H.
Montgomery

THE NEW AMERICANISM

THE NEW AMERICANISM

And Other Speeches and Essays

by
ROBERT WELCH

WITHDRAWN

WESTERN ISLANDS

PUBLISHERS
BOSTON • LOS ANGELES

Paperbound edition published 1976

Published by
WESTERN ISLANDS
Belmont, Massachusetts 02178

Library of Congress Catalog Card Number: 66-26864
ISBN Number: 0-88279-123-0

Manufactured in the United States of America

Contents

Foreword

ROBERT WELCH, if he loved his country less or his comfort more, would today be on a sidewalk in Paris playing a masterly game of chess or on an Oakley fairway playing what he mistakenly calls golf or in an Ivory Tower writing a book about mathematics or nineteenth century poetry. And I would not be writing this introduction but would be writing a piece of my own about the bilious bishop of Ossory and whether his play *King Johan* was produced before Queen Elizabeth in 1561 at Hedingham Castle or in an Ipswich innyard—or some similar exercise of escape from a world gone mad.

Some of my friends will not read this book because Robert Welch wrote it. He, for a variety of trivial and contradictory reasons is, for them, the devil and Joe McCarthy incarnate. They would not read McCarthy's book *America's Retreat from Victory* even after being told that it was in fact written by Forrest Davis, an honest and capable scholar, who had neither horns nor a tail.

Distrust of the author was only an excuse. They were afraid that they could not resist the frightening conclusions of the book and would thus be shaken in mind and troubled in conscience for a day or two before relapsing into their accustomed state of dreamy content.

Robert Welch is a holdover from the "mentally free world of pre-1914." He was educated before John Dewey scuttled the syllogism and before America abandoned the classical curriculum that had brought the Renaissance to England in the sixteenth century and the Constitution to America in the eighteenth. This, according to a definition I claim as my own but probably borrowed from a forgotten source, made him an educated man: He had learned to think and

knew the history of civilization, its rise and fall. This combination of
logic and knowledge makes his books impervious to attack. They cannot be met head-on or even sniped at successfully. They *can* be dis-
torted or misrepresented by the smearbunders and the truth-twisters,
and they can be ignored by the timid denizens of Academe who, to
survive, keep their necks in. (By careful selection of courses and
teachers a student can still get a good education under the inbred
ignorance of the elective system, but it will not be long before the
last old woman who can teach Greek will have joined the gods on
Olympus.)

Although it is a collection of speeches and essays written at different times and for different occasions and purposes, this book is not
fragmentary nor disjointed, but rather has unity and coherence. The
study of civilization and decivilization and the forms and theories of
government from the early B.C.'s in Greece to the early A.D.'s in Rome
prepares us for the enormous fraud and fervid illogic underlying the
French Revolution; and, after that, for the Bolshevik conquest of
Russia; and now for the imminent destruction of the American republic and western civilization—*unless* . . .

But because he took a long time writing it, Mr. Welch has treated
these and other great subjects with admirable brevity and clarity.
The book has the prime requisites of any book. It is readable and interesting.

Robert Welch reveres the American Constitution and places it
high among human achievements and highest among frames of government. He does not quote but would approve Gladstone's assertion that the Constitution of the United States is "the most wonderful work ever struck off at a given time by the brain and purpose of
man." There are men who scoff at the founding fathers and find
them faintly amusing. For them it is considered a devastating appraisal of Robert A. Taft to say that he had the best mind of the
eighteenth century. Of course that is a tremendous compliment. In
the field of government and statecraft the eighteenth century is the
greatest of all the centuries and the founding fathers who met to
draft our Constitution had the greatest minds of that century. Benjamin Franklin was only one of the great men at the convention,

but he understood the Constitution as well as any of them. When the drafting was completed someone asked him, "What have you given us?" He answered, "A republic, if you can keep it."

Well, we kept it for a long time and it worked superbly. What was it that led us to abandon the best form of government ever devised and embrace democracy and the totalitarian tyranny that inevitably follows democracy? It was not a reasoned, debated, political decision. It had no roots in economic nor in social conditions in the United States. The problems we had, if humanly soluble, could have been met by state or local governments or by individuals without wrecking the Constitution and without using evil means. Is there any escape from Robert Welch's conclusions that since 1912, and perhaps before, a criminal conspiracy intent on world conquest and the enslavement of the entire human race has been operating in this country? I hope there is but I have not found it.

Robert Welch's conclusions are frightening but he is not frightened, at least for the long pull. For the short pull his optimism rests on his belief that a majority of Americans like our system and love our country and would do something drastic about the conspiracy if they knew enough about it. As he demonstrates, the conspiracy is by no means invincible. There is a lot of bluff in it that only needs to be called and will be called if the truth can be made known to enough people while there still is time.

ROBERT H. MONTGOMERY
Cambridge, Massachusetts

THE NEW AMERICANISM

The New Americanism

As delivered at a student convocation of Dickinson College, Carlisle, Pennsylvania, in February 1957.

SEVEN HUNDRED YEARS AGO Alfonso of Castile said: "Had I been present at the creation, I would have given some useful hints for the better ordering of the universe." Alfonso was referring specifically to the rather absurd Ptolemaic explanation of our astronomical system. But his intriguing thoughts of personally taking a hand in remaking the world has been an obsession with man since our ancestors began establishing squatter's rights to the most attractive caves. And forty years ago, when I was the age of you young men, I used to quote Omar:

> Ah Love! could you and I with Him conspire
> To grasp this sorry Scheme of Things entire,
>   Would we not shatter it to bits—and then
> Remold it nearer to the Heart's desire!

What each of us has in mind, of course, in making the world over, is not some cosmological purpose in which man is only incidental, but the dreams of man as the center of all consideration. And neither Alfonso nor Omar was thinking of changing *man* to fit better into the framework of his existence; but of changing that *framework*, of "improving" the universe, so that it would be better suited to human beings and their desires.

So let's suppose this morning that an all-powerful Creator has said to you or to me: "All right, here is the very wand of omnipotence, so far as your little universe is concerned. Remake it to suit yourself." What would we do?

Well, let's hope that we would immediately become conscious of the awesome and incredible responsibility; and that before decreeing a morning to break eternal, bright, and fair we would remind ourselves that there are men who like cold climates and some who like the rain. Let's hope we would be seized by such a care for the wishes and beliefs of other men as to constitute an almost infinite sense of *noblesse oblige*. We would then soon decide that before bringing about any changes in this scheme of things we needed the opinions and advice of a lot of our fellow human beings. And we would finally come to the conclusion that the total desires of the whole human race had to be considered before we should try to make everything for the best in the best of all possible worlds.

Our first solicitude, therefore, before we started flashing the lightnings or rolling the suns, would have to be over man's sociological organizations on this planet. We would need to arrive at, or to see established, a system of government or governments that would be most responsive to man's most carefully and deliberately indicated wishes; that would offer each man the best opportunity to get out of his own life the most possible of what he himself believed to be most worthwhile; and that would enable the whole race of men to decide wisely, or at least fairly, what changes should be made in their physical environment. Our very first job would be to determine the kind, the quality, and the quantity of government that best serves man's needs for the present and aspirations for the future. This would have to be done, and such government or governments provided, before we could, in good conscience, make a single move with our wand towards otherwise reordering the universe nearer to man's desire.

So our supposing has now brought us to the task of writing or planning a Utopia. Since it is simpler and safer to deal with one variable at the time in any equation, this Utopia should be planned for our physical universe *as it now is*. From this start, if and as changes in the physical setting were to be made later, we could then consider the adjustment in our sociological pattern called for by such changes. And in designing the first stage of this Utopia, therefore, for earth and mankind as they now are, we should certainly make the best possible use of man's past experience.

Now we are quite aware of Hegel's generalization that we learn nothing from history except that we learn nothing from history. We have often quoted Santayana's deduction from that lament, that those who will learn nothing from history are condemned to repeat it. But why? Why must we, as a race, close our eyes to all or so much that experience can teach us, or to all the mistakes of the past, and go on making those same mistakes as if our civilization had come into existence only yesterday? It seems to me that this is an unnecessary absurdity; that there is no biological compulsion for us to be so stupid; and that the very first barrier man must cross, in order to travel towards a Utopia, is this unwillingness to be guided by the clear lessons of his own past. To assume that either man or his environment has changed so much during his recorded history that these lessons of the past no longer apply, is not only unrealistic; it is a childish fantasy that gives a fairy-tale quality to our most labored thoughts.

II

On the basis of all known past human experience, therefore, are there any general conclusions with regard to societal organization which can be postulated with confidence? It seems to me that there certainly are.

1. First, government is necessary—some degree of government —in any civilized society. There are believers in the possibility and desirability of a governmentless anarchy as a practicable form of human association. But the number of these advocates

is comparatively very small, there is no evidence within human historical experience to support their thesis, and there is considerable evidence indicating otherwise.

2. Second, while government is necessary, it is basically a nonproductive expense, an overhead cost supported by the productive economy. And like all overhead items, it always has a tendency to expand faster than the productive base which supports it.

3. Third, government is frequently evil. And we do not mean by this that they (governments) are merely dishonest. For all governments, with very rare exceptions indeed, are thoroughly dishonest. We made the statement in print, a few months ago, that there has never in the history of the world been a government (and this generalization includes our present one) that maintained honesty in the handling of a "managed" irredeemable currency. A few weeks later one of America's ablest and best-known economists quoted that statement with full approval.

But what we are talking about here is something far worse than dishonesty. This past December Professor Sorokin of Harvard—after quoting Lord Acton that great men, in the political arena, are almost always bad men—went on to reveal the results of his own survey of the criminality of rulers. This survey of the monarchs of various countries and the heads of various republics and democracies, in a selection large enough to constitute a very fair sample, revealed that there was an average of one murderer to every four of these rulers. "In other words," says Professor Sorokin, "the rulers of the states are the most criminal group in a respective population. With a limitation of their power their criminality tends to decrease; but it still remains exceptionally high in all nations."

An obvious reason for this is the greater temptation to criminality on the part of those who control or influence the police power of a nation, of which they would otherwise stand in more fear. Another is that ambitious men with criminal tendencies naturally gravitate into government because of this very prospect of doing, or helping to do, the policing over themselves. A third reason is that so many apologists can always be found, for criminal acts of governments, on the grounds that such acts ultimately contribute to the public good and that therefore the criminal means are justified by the righteous ends. Kautilya wrote his *Arthashastra* in about 300 B.C. Machiavelli wrote his *Il Principe* in about 1500 A.D. And the arguments of both, that it is a virtue in a ruler to be unscrupulous for the good of his state, are heard in every age.

4. Fourth, government is always and inevitably an enemy of individual freedom. It seems rather strange that it was Woodrow Wilson, who more than any other one man started this nation on its present road towards totalitarianism, who also said that the history of human liberty is a history of the limitations of governmental power, not the increase of it. But Wilson could have boasted, as did Charles II of England, that he said only wise things even though he did only foolish ones. It is self-evident that government, by its very nature, *must* be an enemy of freedom, edging always towards a restriction of the individual's rights and responsibilities.

5. Whatever must be done by governments will always cost more than if it could be done by individuals or smaller groups. And the larger the government, the more disproportionate will be the cost. Letting a government do anything, therefore, which such individuals or smaller groups could properly do, is serious economic wastefulness. It is also contrary to the philosophy of the proper function of government that is derived from the whole body of past experiments.

6. Government, by its size, its momentum, and its authority, will not only perpetuate errors of doctrine or of policy longer than they would otherwise retain acceptance, but it will multiply their effect on a geometric scale, as against the arithmetically cumulative effect of those errors if confined to individuals or smaller groups. The errors of tens of thousands of individuals, all thinking and probing in different directions and moved by different impulses, tend to cancel themselves out or to be softened by the attrition of doubt and disagreement. But let any one error become sanctified by government, and thus crystallized as truth,

and little short of a revolution can discredit it or cause it to be discarded.

An easy illustration of this principle is the witchcraft terror in the early days of the colonial government of Massachusetts. If there had been no governmental power to give phantasmagoria the semblance of reality by official decree, the common sense of a majority of the citizens would have kept this manifestation of fanaticism from ever having such widespread support and cruel results. But once government had authoritatively said, "This is truth," then the hitherto doubting citizen was willing to join others like himself in accepting it as truth. And we have at least a dozen idiocies, equally repugnant to man's common sense and sound experience, being perpetuated by our government in Washington today. But it would take as long a book to convince most people of the absurdity and harmfulness of any one of them as it would have taken to convince the citizens of Salem, Massachusetts, in 1692, of the nonsense of their belief in witchcraft, once government had guaranteed the wisdom of that belief.

7. As any society becomes reasonably settled, and shakes down into a semi-permanent pattern of economic and political life, and as some degree of leisure on the part of its citizens becomes both possible and visible, the drive always begins to have government become the management of the social enterprise rather than merely its agent for certain clear purposes. Government is then increasingly allowed, invited, and even urged to do planning for, and exercise control over, the total economy of the nation. Next, it is pushed, and pushes itself, more and more into planning and control of the separate activities of the citizens and groups of citizens that make up the economic life of the nation. And in doing such planning and exercising such controls the government must assume more and more of the responsibility for the success of the economy and the welfare of its citizens.

Of course no government, short of being omniscient, can ever plan the specialized division of labor and the beneficial interchange of the various products of human effort, or can ever appraise the impact of changing circumstances and changing desires on the infinite ramifications of interrelated human activity, one half as well as the planning, appraisal, and resulting corrections will be accomplished by a completely free market if given the opportunity. For the free market automatically weighs, measures, and integrates into its decisions increments of need, of difficulty, and of motivation that are too small, too numerous, and too hidden for the planners ever to discover them. And the equations to be dealt with are too infinite to be resolved by any human brain or committee of human brains, even if all the variables and constants could be accurately set forth in such equations.

A government trying to step in and improve the workings of a free market is exactly like a man who takes a lantern outdoors at noon of a bright June day to show you the sun. But a government's answer to any criticism as to the inadequacy of the lantern is always to bring more lanterns and then more lanterns—until eventually the smoke and glare of the lanterns so seriously interfere with and shut off the light of the sun that everybody actually has to work mainly by lantern light.

It is interesting to note, too, that in any society the government, and its allies who want to use the lanterns, always claim the justification that the society's economy is more complex than those which have preceded it. They insist that therefore the lanterns of planning and control are necessary and helpful now, no matter how futile and harmful they have been shown to be in the past. Of course exactly the opposite is true. The more complex the economic life of a nation becomes; the more nearly infinite the shades and grades of impulse which determine the proper interchanges and relationships between its components become; then the more impossible and ridiculous is any undertaking to plan and control those relationships, and the more the automatic working of a completely free market is needed.

8. As a government increases in power, and as a means of increasing its power, it always has a tendency to squeeze out the middle class; to destroy or weaken the middle for the benefit of the top and the bottom. Even where there is no conscious alliance

for this purpose, such as formed the basis for Bismarck's beginning of the socialization of Germany or Franklin Roosevelt's beginning of the socialization of America, the forces to that end are always at work—as they have been in England for fifty years. In the nations that the gods would destroy, they first make the middle class helpless through insidious but irresistible government pressures.

9. The form of government is not nearly so important as its quality. Justice and a lack of arbitrariness, for instance, are two characteristics of a government that are most important to the welfare and happiness of a people. They are as likely to be found—or more accurately, as little likely to be found—under any one form of government as another. Rampant interference with personal lives is the most obnoxious characteristic of any government, and that is found just as readily under elected officials as under hereditary monarchs. In fact, as the Greeks pointed out, as has been well known to careful students of history ever since, and as the founding fathers of our own republic were well aware, when an elected government succeeds in attracting and maintaining an overwhelming majority behind it for any length of time, its mob instincts make it the most tyrannical of all forms of social organization.

10. Which brings us to the last, the most overlooked, and in my opinion the most important, of these basic generalizations concerning government. Thomas Jefferson expressed part of it in his famous dictum that that government is best which governs least. But Jefferson was thinking of the extent of a government's power more than of the extensiveness of the government itself. And our tenth point is that neither the form of government nor its quality is as important as its quantity. A thoroughly foul government, like that of Nero, which still did not reach its tentacles too far into the daily lives and doings of its subjects, was far better for the Roman Empire in the long run than the intentionally benevolent government of Diocletian or of Constantine, whose bureaucratic agents were everywhere. Let's dramatize this fact—or opinion—by bringing it closer home. And your

speaker would like to have it understood that he does not condone dishonesty in the slightest degree. Yet I had rather have
for America, and I am convinced America would be better off
with, a government of three hundred thousand officials and
agents, every single one of them a thief, than a government of
three million agents with every single one of them an honest,
honorable, public servant. For the first group would only steal
from the American economic and political system; the second
group would be bound in time to destroy it. *The increasing
quantity of government, in all nations, has constituted the
greatest tragedy of the twentieth century.*

Let's spotlight just one particular result of this tragic development which has occurred in connection with man's age-old
worry—war. That result is the frequency, the length, the extensiveness, the horrible destructiveness, and the totality of impact on the population, of the wars of the twentieth century.
In the physical sciences we are accustomed to using combined
measurements, such as foot-pounds, kilowatt-hours or man-days.
Let's invent such a phrase for the measurement of war, and
call it the day-number-horror unit. In the use of that three-way
calculation we multiply the days of suffering by the number of
people who suffer by the depth of the suffering, to arrive at an
appraisal. Then I believe you will find that pretty generally
throughout history—despite other factors causing occasional exceptions—and very definitely throughout recent centuries, the
day-number-horrors measure of any war has been proportional
to the contemporary extensiveness of government. In fact and
specifically, it has been directly proportional to the *product* of
the *quantities* of government in the nations involved at the time
a war was fought.

Also, you will find that it is the huge quantity of government
which, more than anything else, makes these tremendously destructive wars not only possible, but unavoidable. One illustration should make this statement too clear for argument. Do *you*
want to fight the Russian people? Do you think the Russian
people have the least desire to fight us? Do you think there

would be the slightest chance of the American people and the Russian people fighting each other, with millions to be killed on both sides and great parts of both countries probably to be utterly destroyed, if there were only one-tenth as much government in each country as now exists? Stop and think about it for a minute. It is not only that governments carry their peoples into horrible and utterly unnecessary wars, but it takes a very huge quantity of government to carry its people into the totalitarian struggle which war has now been made by this same quantity of government. Reduce all the governments of all the nations of the world to one-third of their present size—not one-third of their power, note, nor are we referring to their quality, but just to one-third of their bureaucratic numbers, their extensiveness, their meddling in the lives of their subjects—and you would immediately accomplish two things. You would reduce the likelihood of war between hostile nations to at most one-ninth of its present probability, and the destructiveness of any wars that did take place in the same proportion.

The greatest enemy of man is, and always has been, government. And the larger, the more extensive that government, the greater the enemy.

III

Now, you may well be asking, what on earth does all of this have to do with the announced subject of my speech, "The New Americanism"? But I hope that the connection will soon become clear.

For Americanism, as either a phrase or a force on the contemporary world scene, has been eroded into something negative and defeatist. It has come to represent merely a delaying action against the victorious march of its enemy, collectivism. The air is full of clarion calls to Americans to organize, in order better to fight *against* socialism, communism, or some vanguard of their forces. Twice each day the mail brings to my desk pleas for me to contribute money, or effort, or moral support, or all three, to some group which is battling to hold back some particular advance of collectivist storm troops. Even those organizations or activities which bear a positive label are motivated by negative thinking. An association *for* the Bricker amendment is, in reality, an association *against* the intervention of international socialist forces in the control of our domestic lives. Americanism has become primarily a denial of something else, rather than an assertion of itself. And there are many of us who think that this should be true no longer. We think that Americanism should again come to mean, and to be, a positive, forward-looking philosophy; a design and example of social organization which boldly and confidently offers leadership along the one hard but sure road to a better world. And it was necessary to explore and emphasize these fundamental truths about government as a background to any discussion of "The New Americanism."

It is not just in the United States, of course, that all the aggressiveness is on the side of the socialist-communist allies. In the worldwide ideological struggle which divides mankind today, we conservatives fight always on the defensive. The very name by which we identify ourselves defines our objective. It is to conserve as much as we can, out of all we have inherited that is worthwhile, from the encroachments and destructiveness of this advancing collectivism. We build no more icons to freedom; we merely try to fend off the iconoclast.

Such has been the pattern during the whole first half of the twentieth century. From the bright plateaux of individual freedom and individual responsibility which man had precariously attained there has been a steady falling back towards the dark valleys of dependence and serfdom. But this ignominious retreat has been just as true of Americans, the heirs of a strong new society, as of the tired residual legatees of an old and enfeebled European civilization. During this long and forced retreat we have fought only a rearguard and sometimes delaying action. We have never been rallied to counterattack, to break through the enemy or rout him, and to climb again beyond our highest previous gains. And in the unending skirmishes, to hold as much as possible of the ground currently occupied, we have lost all sight of the higher tablelands of freedom which once were our recognized goals. I for one, and many others like me, are no longer willing to consider only when to retreat and how far. There is a braver and a wiser course.

If we heirs of all the ages are to find a turning point in this rapid and sometimes stampeding descent, in which we are abandoning instead of improving our inheritance; if the last half of the twentieth century is to see the curve that measures individual dignity turn upward; if the men who really wish to be free and self-reliant are to begin climbing back up the mountainside; then the goal must be known, and the purpose of aggressive offense must replace defensive defeatism as the banner under which we march. It is fatal to be merely against losing ground, for then there is no way to go but back. We have to be *for* something; we must know what that something is; and we must believe it is worth a fight to obtain. And a great deal of what we are for can be summarized as simply increasing freedom from the tentacles of government.

There are many of us who want America and Americans to take the lead in this fight so vigorously, and to establish so clearly as their goal those new heights of personal freedom never before reached, that the whole worldwide positive forward movement can be identified and will be identified as americanism. We want the very word americanism, with a little "a," to come to mean not the jingoistic and provincial outlook of a certain geographical area, but a philosophy of freedom to which the courageous and the self-reliant everywhere can subscribe. We want "an americanist" to come to mean any man, no matter in what country he lives, who believes in and supports this philosophy. Although Russia is the alma mater of communism, and a large percentage of all communists are inhabitants of Russia, the word communist may designate a citizen of any other country just as readily as a Russian. We should like to see Americans earn the right and the glory to have the true anti-communists everywhere designate themselves as americanists. Due to the tremendous momentum given us by our hard-working, ambitious, and individualistic forefathers, our nation is still by far the most dynamic in the world in its productive processes, and in its influences on the whole world's standard of living. We must again become equally dynamic in our *spiritual* influence; in our positive leadership and example to provide a governmental environment in which individual man can make the most of his life in whatever way *he*—and not his government—wishes to use it.

There are many stages of welfarism, socialism, and collectivism in general, but communism is the ultimate stage of them all, and they all lead inevitably in that direction. In this final stage, communism, you have a society in which class distinctions are greater than in any other, but where position in these classes is determined solely by demagogic political skill and ruthless cunning. You have a society in which all those traits which have helped to make man civilized, and which our multiple faiths have classified as virtues, are now discarded as vices—while exactly their opposites are glorified. And you have a society in which every *fault* of government that we have discussed above is held to be a *benefit* and a desirable part of the framework of life.

But there is an exactly opposite direction. It leads towards a society in which brotherhood and kindliness and tolerance and honesty and self-reliance and the integrity of the human personality are considered virtues; a society which venerates those traits exactly because they have helped the human animal to achieve some degree of humanitarian civilization, and are the common denominators of all our great religions. This direction leads towards a governmental environment for human life founded on the basis of long experience with government; on experience which shows government to be a necessary evil, but a continuous brake on all progress and the ultimate enemy of all freedom. It is the forward direction, the upward direction—and americanism, I hope, shall become its name.

IV

For this brings us back, Gentlemen, to our game of supposing; to the wand of omnipotence hypothetically handed to us at the beginning of this speech. And now I can explain, if you did not already guess it, that this is no day dream, and the wand I had in mind is not imaginary. It is very real, and we already have it. Man is already able to create heat where there was cold and cold where there was heat; rain where there was drought and desert where there was swamp; valleys where there were mountains and mountains where there were valleys. He has already reached the point that he could create islands to run around the northern hemisphere, above the clouds and at seven hundred miles per hour—the same speed at which the earth's surface turns under the sun. This means that those who inhabited such islands could dwell in a perpetual sunrise, or actually live in a morning that breaks eternal, bright, and fair—if they so desired. Man already has the physical power and the scientific knowledge to convert this whole planet into a garden, or to blow it to smithereens. Which he does will depend largely on *you*, and other young people like you. And that is why I am here this morning.

While this short talk may strengthen the resolution of the comparatively few among you who are already americanists—whether you accept the term or not—it is not likely to make any converts among those whom I can almost hear object; who are now scornfully formulating in their own minds their disbelief and disagreement with regard to all that I have said. I do not expect it to do so. I hope only to stir a questioning among you, a willingness to search for the truth more objectively and more independently than you may perhaps have searched in the past.

For among this generation of students there has been a tragic loss of the honest spirit of intellectual inquisitiveness. Where on earth is, what has happened to, the so-called rebelliousness of youth, especially in our colleges? What I am saying now may not apply so much to you at Dickinson, as elsewhere. I hope and believe that it does not. But on the whole, throughout the classrooms of a thousand American campuses the college youth of today are willing to accept almost without question, abide by, and militantly support, the most deadly intellectual conformity that has ever been imposed on similar numbers of men and women of similar intelligence and opportunity. And the fact that the stale blanket of collectivist doctrine is conspicuously labeled "revolutionary" while it is being spread blindingly over their minds is no justification for their meek acquiescence. The dwellers in our colleges and universities for centuries past have always been, or have been supposed to be, independent, curious, skeptical, courageous seekers after truth; not indifferent mental softies, herded like a bunch of sheep into a corral of conformity just by the trick of putting a false sign on the gate.

So I am saying to you simply this. Find out for yourselves You don't have to accept my beliefs, my interpretation of his tory, nor my ideas of what should be done to put the human race in the best position to use its wand of near-omnipotence. But for goodness' sake do not meekly or lazily accept the ideas, slants, and conclusions of the collectivist conformists either. And above all, do not ignore the experience accumulated by two hundred generations of your ancestors. Study the past, analyze the present, and dream the future for yourselves. By the time you discover that communism is just a new version of Spartan fascism, even to the cunning and cruelty by which it is maintained; that modern collectivist theory is just warmed-over Plato; that time after time men have abandoned all home ties and migrated to new lands just to escape the very tyranny of too much government that is now closing in on us again; and that man's progress, spiritual as well as material, has almost always been inversely proportional to the amount of government control over his actions; by the time you find out these things for yourself—as you surely will if you study history diligently and objectively enough—I think you will join that rising force of americanists who are determined that americanism shall again become a beacon for mankind.

A Letter to Khrushchev

This open letter first appeared in the April 1958 issue of American Opinion, *an informal monthly review edited by Robert Welch.*

March 3, 1958

NIKITA S. KHRUSHCHEV
The Kremlin, Moscow, USSR

Sir:

FIRST, we apologize for using the worn-out technique of the "open letter." It is the only apology you will find anywhere in these pages.

We are publishing this message, instead of merely mailing it to you, however, for two reasons. (A) We hope it will be endorsed by an appreciable number of anti-Communists in this country as a crystallization of some of their own thoughts. (B) The chance of having it actually read and considered by yourself will be much increased by this procedure. We want it to come to your attention—and, frankly, we believe that it will.

Do Not Expect Diplomatic Language . . .

Second, our phrasing will be straightforward. Using words, not to convey thoughts, but to disguise them, was in Talleyrand's time only a formula. The practice has now become a major branch of our contemporary arts and sciences. So the communications which you receive through diplomatic channels from officials of our government would seldom assay one brass tack to the carload. It may be well worthwhile for you to read a letter from an American private citizen, who can tell you what he thinks without swaddling the substance irretrievably in hypocritical humbug.

As a part of that straightforwardness, we shall not go out of our way to be insulting, as you have frequently done in addressing us—making a grandstand play of the insult for its propaganda value. Nor shall we, on the other hand, either make any pretense of hiding our dislike for you and your associates, or sidestep the use of pungent idiom if it accurately expresses our point of view. A major reason for writing this letter is to speak, so far as we can, for that segment of the American population —which we believe still to be the preponderant majority— that is basically and bitterly hostile to your whole regime, and that feels betrayed by all of the expressions and manifestations of friendship towards you on the part of our present administration in Washington. Our government, following a proverbial principle of politicians, may well have hinted: "If you will desist from telling lies about us, we will refrain from telling the truth about you." But this writer does not subscribe to any such undertaking.

BUT PLAIN TRUTH, AT FIRST HAND . . .

Third, we are aware that you have plenty of agents in our midst whose duties include the continuous despatch back to the Kremlin of detailed reports as to what the American people are thinking. But agents can be deceived, or deceiving. And anyway, you can save the cost of a lot of microfilm by simply reading this issue of *American Opinion*. You will not even have to buy a copy. A gift subscription, to start with this number, has been entered for you by an enemy of yours. That's how we got the inspiration for this letter. Giving you some unvarnished truth might conceivably dispel a few dangerous ideas which may be chasing each other around in your sometimes vodka-soaked upper story. Just for instance, you could be starting to believe some of your own propaganda. And that would be a bad mistake. For remember: If an erstwhile pal of yours named Hitler had paid less attention to his yes-men, and listened more attentively to some of his American *foes*, he might be dining on Wiener schnitzel in Berchtesgaden tonight.

Finally, this writer—along with many of his friends—does not believe that you are the "head of state" in Russia today at all. We think you are a "front" man, told what to say and how to say it, when to clown and when to rant, by Malenkov—or whoever the real dictator may be—behind the scenes. But we are perfectly willing to go along with this imposture and address our remarks to you as if you really were the boss. For we deduce that yours is one of the most important sets of ears, as well as tongues and sets of hands, at his disposal. So we hope you will listen, both for him and for yourself.

II

Strange to say, most of what we have to tell you is going to please you very much. For example, we know that you are winning the cold war by leaps and bounds. We are familiar with the three-step program laid out by Lenin for the Communist conquest of the world: First, eastern Europe, then the masses of Asia, and last the final bastion of opposition, the United States of America. We can see that you have already completed the first step entire, three-fourths of the second step, and—through the power of your strategically placed agents—at least one-fourth of the last step. In fact, we measured your tremendous geographical progress, in some detail, in an article entitled "Look at the Score," in the November 1957 issue of this magazine. (Back copies, each, fifty cents American or one thousand kopecks.) We are duly impressed and honestly frightened by that score.

We Know about Your Agents in Our Government . . .

We also acknowledge the remarkable degree of your influence in, or control over, a huge number of the governments of the world, even those outside of the Iron Curtain—and most assuredly including our own. We think that when Stalin implied to the Czech diplomat Arnhost Heidrich in 1947 that he, Stalin, was even then in practical control of the American government (see the *Saturday Evening Post*, July 14, 1947), he was not exaggerating. We think that this control of the Kremlin over the policies and actions of our government has steadily increased and tightened during the ten years since.

We are sure that a very high percentage of the individuals in our government are entirely loyal and patriotic public servants. Nevertheless this whole organization has been insidiously but steadily led down the road the Kremlin wanted it to follow by a clever and powerful minority of manipulators—consisting of actual Communist agents, Communist sympathizers, and their socialist allies and dupes. Loyal individuals, in positions of any authority at all, who were not gulled as to the direction the whole body was traveling, had to be willing to close their eyes to that direction instead of opposing the movement. Otherwise they soon found themselves transferred to less important positions, or on the outside altogether. And we think that the number, prestige, power, and brazenness of your agents within our government today, at all levels, is by far the greatest it has ever been. Many of our readers have heard us say this before, but not in a letter to you, so we hope they will forgive the repetition.

And What They Have Accomplished . . .

We recognize the many disastrous steps our government, or the political masters of our destinies, have taken during the last decade, as a result of this control from the Kremlin, to help international Communism. Regardless of the plausible excuses, oblique approaches, and indirect wire-pulling through which that control was exercised, many of the results have been catastrophic for our best friends throughout the world as well as for ourselves. Among the most important of these pro-Communist actions, or Communist-aiding activities, during the past twelve years—even though some did not seem so at the time to many who participated in them—are the following:

ABROAD . . .

(1) The betrayal of our great ally Mihailovich, and the turning of Yugoslavia over to Stalin's hatchet man Tito—as fully documented in David Martin's *Ally Betrayed*.

(2) The betrayal of Poland by the Acheson-dominated State Department, and the turning of that country over to Stalin's Lublin Gang—as accurately described by our own ambassador right on the spot, Arthur Bliss Lane, in his book *I Saw Poland Betrayed*.

(3) The betrayal of Chiang Kai-shek, and the turning of the mainland of China over to your murderous subordinate Mao Tse-tung by the Dean Acheson-Alger Hiss-George Marshall axis in our State Department—as fully disclosed in George Creel's *Russia's Race for Asia* and a dozen other books.

(4) The dismissal of General MacArthur in order to keep him from winning the Korean War.

OR AT HOME . . .

(5) The snatching of the Republican nomination from Taft in 1952 by purchase, theft, secret deals, and other tactics more foul than had ever before appeared in American politics. For Taft, as you well knew, would have cleaned out your agents by the thousands, and had to be defeated at any cost.

(6) The negotiations at Panmunjom, where all of the negotiators on the Communist side, all of the "neutralists" like

Nehru, and entirely too many of the negotiators on our side were working for the Kremlin.

(7) The defeat of the Bricker amendment, which would have constituted a roadblock across the flow of American sovereignty and power of decision into the United Nations, ILO, NATO, and other international organizations.

(8) The Supreme Court decision of May 17, 1954, with the ultimate purpose (on your part, anyway) of fomenting civil war in this country.

(9) The censure by the United States Senate of Joe McCarthy—of which most of the senators who were pressured and bamboozled into so asinine a slap at themselves are now (when it is much too late) thoroughly ashamed.

(10) Our huge (and still continuing) part in the surrender of French Indochina to the Communists.

AND ALSO HOW . . .

(11) The constant catering of our government to Communist collaborators, "neutralists," and viceroys like Gronchi of Italy, Nehru of India, and Sukarno of Indonesia—the last of whom, a Communist stooge all of his adult life, and who only a few years before had led in the streets of Batavia a mob that burned an American president in effigy as an "imperialist," was in 1955 accorded the longest and most fulsome "state" visit in our nation's history. (As if you didn't know, or how it was arranged.)

(12) The "Summit Conference" in Geneva in 1955, which could have and did have no possible result except the strengthening of the Kremlin's grip inside the Iron Curtain and the aggrandizement of its prestige abroad.

(13) The double-crossing by agencies of our government of the East German uprising in 1953 and of the Hungarian uprising in 1956.

(14) The acceptance by our National Security Council of

the official position that we want the satellite nations to remain as military allies of Soviet Russia.

(15) The whole gigantic hoax called NATO, inaugurated by Dean Acheson, started on its way by the Communist-dominated Truman administration, and built to its present incredible mountain of extravagant futility by the influence of your agents in our government and other governments of the West.

(16) The whole Sputnik episode with all of its ramifications, of which we shall have more to say anon.

WE DO NOT CONGRATULATE YOU, BUT . . .

You are doing all right, Comrade Khrushchev; very much all right from your point of view. And we are well aware that the speed of your progress, the arrogant openness of the help given you by our government, and the vicious crushing of your opposition everywhere (including inside America) have all greatly increased since 1953. We are not happy about it, but we are realistic enough to face the facts.

We know that you know all of these things, Comrade Khrushchev, but a third step is important. We want you to know that we know that you know. We have recounted some of the far-reaching maneuvers which have herded us to this precipice because we wanted to convince you that the Kremlin's hidden hand in those maneuvers was not as hidden as you might have hoped. By the time we come to write the final and most important paragraphs of this letter, we must have made clear: (1) that we really do know how far you have already gone towards making the United States just another batch of three or four Soviet republics; and (2) that we understand the methods and the measures by which you have achieved such staggering results. In that vein, and for that purpose, let's turn from the past to what is happening right now, and to what you thoroughly expect to happen in the proximate future.

III

In the first place, we are sure that your former agent Igor Gouzenko was absolutely right when he said that your success in launching the earth satellite Sputnik was due to two factors: (1) the theft of the know-how from various agencies of our Defense Department; and (2) the deliberate holding back of such a launching by ourselves through the influence of treason at work in our government. The treasonous moves were, as Gouzenko says, disguised under seemingly logical excuses. But the net result, and the intended result, was to let you have the glory, the propaganda value, and all of the less obvious advantages of this first conquest of outer space.

Even the obtainable evidence to support this assertion is plentiful, and has been for a long time. In a speech by Senator McCarthy as far back as October 1955—on a platform which this writer shared with him as the only other speaker—the senator pointed out that our own progress in the field of missile and rocket production was being willfully slowed down by traitorous forces inside our government. And he prophesied exactly what has now happened, as bound to happen unless the treason was rooted out.

YOU FLOATED YOUR SPUTNIK . . .

We are not overlooking the importance of your kidnapped German scientists, Comrade Khrushchev, for many of them were and are rocket specialists. With their knowledge and experience, plus the information stolen from us—both directly and through the British—plus a "crash program" at any cost, you were able to put a ball high enough above the earth's atmosphere to have it settle into a tentative and temporary orbit. You even followed that up with a second ball, supposedly much larger—but concerning which all specifications and reports have been much less authentically confirmed. And we are con-

vinced that you also can justly claim credit for the way we
have been so pantingly playing second fiddle, and shouting
"Look, me too," ever since.

But we are further convinced, Comrade Khrushchev, largely
by your own claims to having such a plethora of rockets and
missiles ready to loose on our helpless heads, that you do not
have any such thing. For we know from long observation how
your mind and your strategy work. If you really did have the
weapons and the superiority in advanced technology to accomplish our destruction or to be sure of winning any war that got
started, you would be telling us just the opposite until you
were ready to start using the weapons.

As You Got the Bomb . . .

We believe that there is a close parallel here with your former
actions and pretenses in connection with nuclear weapons. We
do not doubt either the knowledge, or the accuracy of the conclusion, of the former chief of security training of our whole
governmental enterprise in the field of atomic energy. He says
that up until 1953, at least, in all probability you had never
manufactured even one atomic bomb; that those which you
had been "test-exploding" for show-off purposes you had assembled out of parts which your agents had easily stolen, and
simply walked away with, from our plants. And we think that,
similarly, all of your claims to solid scientific accomplishment
based on the Sputnik stunt are one-third exaggeration and two-
thirds sheer poppycock.

But Your Reputation Is Tough on Your Pretenses . . .

From the past actions of yourself and your associates, it
seems likely that your beeping moonlet was a glittering sample,
contrived at an all-out cost for the display window, with nothing in stock behind it but an exhausted shop. Otherwise, why
would you go to such extreme lengths, through every pipe in

your propaganda organ, to convince us of the opposite. Many of us have read enough Russian history, Comrade Khrushchev, to remember Potemkin's "prosperous" villages on the Dnieper. The houses were only false fronts, without walls or floors behind them, which served the single purpose of making a good show for Catherine and her courtiers as the royal barges floated by. With some cardboard painted to look like tile, and a traveling troupe of actors dressed like peasants, Potemkin gave Catherine a deluded glimpse of a whole happy empire in the Crimea. With one missile weighing—so it is claimed—165 pounds, and another one much more vaguely presented for our imaginations to endow with some frightening statistics, you would have us visualize behind them a flotilla of space ships ready to head for Mars. And we are to take for granted that, just as a by-product of building your Sputniks, or vice versa, you have or will soon have a battery of intercontinental missiles ready to pinpoint Times Square, the Boston State House, and Capitol Hill as targets from five thousand miles away. Pfui! We don't claim your grapes are sour, Comrade Khrushchev. Knowing what an inveterate liar you are, we don't believe they even exist.

INFANTRY YOU HAVE . . .

Don't get us wrong. We know that you have a land army massive enough and brutal enough to overrun all of Europe at will—mowing down in the process tens of thousands of our soldiers who have been scattered everywhere in helpless small detachments to make that particular result easier for you. We know that the strongest part of your navy is your fleet of submarines, because submarines were a specialty of the German scientists whom you enslaved in 1945—with the utterly disgraceful assent of representatives of our government. One reason that we really believe in those submarines is that the information comes from authoritative sources *outside* of *your* government or *ours*. Another is that we haven't heard you boasting about them. We are also painfully aware that you do not have to transport your nuclear pilferage to Russia; that it is possible for your agents to steal the parts of, assemble, and hide right here in our cities, enough atomic bombs to do tremendous damage in a surprise attack at any time you felt safe enough from retaliation to undertake one. But the key to all of the problems thus posed for us is really our internal security against treason, not your military strength or ours—and that is the significant point of this discussion to which we are coming in due course.

But Production You Haven't . . .

Also, please do not get us wrong about another matter. We do not claim that Russians are constitutionally incapable of designing a submarine or a rocket. What we doubt so confidently is that you have either the vast technological competence or productive capacity, below the experimental level, to turn out all of those missiles and nuclear bombs you are threatening to start tossing around. The most dependable conclusions, arrived at by the most objective scholars from combining all of the evidence available, is that your equipment, your degree of mechanization, and your production per man-hour, even in your most industrialized centers at their best, are about equal to what ours were in 1920; and that your total industrial production in proportion to your total population is today at the level of ours in 1900!

Your real pride, Comrade Khrushchev, as distinguished from your deceptive boastings to frighten a gullible public, is in the six thousand Communist schools and colleges throughout the world teaching *political* warfare, agitation, and subversion. We know that too large a percentage of the Communist youth, with the best brains and the most ambition, are taking this road to personal advancement for the total inventive genius and technological capacity of your whole brainwashed gang to exceed the level which this country passed right after World War I. As late as 1944, under the most pressing need imaginable, your thousands of brilliant young technologists didn't have "scientific" sense enough to put together the complete manufacturing plants which we shipped them, or to keep such plants running even after we assembled and started them off in good order. Why should we think that in a dozen years your whole engineering and technical-labor population has suddenly moved from the abacus to the electronic-computer stage of dealing with matters mathematical and materials scientific?

FOR SUBVERSION IS YOUR REAL WEAPON . . .

We think you are making headway, without question. And that in due course, if we all live that long, the growing and spreading skill of your workers in technical production processes will move you up from the 1920 notch to some reasonably contemporary level, and one very dangerous for ourselves. But up to now, Comrade Khrushchev, you have been running too many schools and agencies of subversion, because that is the area in which you were winning all of your important victories —and where you are still looking for your decisive victories today. Most of the successful sycophants and brilliant schemers in your system have learned the professional uses of animal cunning and the forensic employment of dialectic cleverness; not how to split an atom—nor how to improve a lathe. In the proper setting of a loaded debating society on the East River, they can lift the wings of logic. But when it comes to lifting the wings of lead, they still have to steal the blueprints from the West, and ape the motions of the West in trying to build and run the machines those blueprints forecast.

AND YOUR BLUFFS ARE SUPERB . . .

If you really have all of this scientific superiority you are beating your breast about, Comrade Khrushchev, why is the basic textbook on nuclear physics which is in use everywhere in the Soviet Union one that was written in, and simply taken from, the United States? Why did you claim that your ten-billion electron-volt atom smasher had reached full power last spring, when it is in this case a known fact that it produced only *one-millionth* as many protons as needed to use it *for research*? And why, pray tell, when you needed in October 1957 to release a picture of your Sputnik to the world for propaganda purposes, did it turn out to be an *exact* reproduction of the photograph of a satellite model on page 129 of the January 1956 issue of our magazine *Popular Science*? Pfui again, Comrade Khrushchev. The *Wall Street Journal*, from which we got a part of the information above, calls you a *truth-stretcher* with regard to your scientific accomplishments. We would offer that, in any contest, as the prize understatement of at least a thousand years.

IV

However, you did get Sputnik I, and even something you could call Sputnik II, up in the sky. And great was the propaganda value thereof. The immediate acclaim, fanned by your agents everywhere, was so great that most people assumed the direct visible results of this *tour de force* to be the most important results. These included: (1) the sheer glory of scientific achievement, and the mighty boost to Russian prestige all over the world which accompanied this glory; (2) the vague fear of what more deadly "machines of the future" you might unloose, on the part of the man in the street everywhere, as expressed by one of them who said, "It sorta gives you the shivers to think of that thing circling around overhead"; and (3) the blackmail value in diplomatic circles of your superiority in advanced weapons, of which this stunt was supposed to be the proof. Your plans to use the phychological advantages thus given you to bring about a "neutralization" of all of Germany were outlined by one of our associate editors, Mr. Schlamm, in the February issue of this magazine.

This harvest alone would constitute a very good return on

your investment. But we think you have some larger and longer schemes afoot, concerned primarily with ourselves, for which the launching of Sputnik was the starting gun. And you do not expect Americans, even a majority of those most active in promoting these schemes for you, to suspect that they are being cleverly inspired and steered into the final destruction of their own republic by your smooth secret agents and your plausible propaganda. For these same "naive Americans" are not yet even aware of how completely our domestic plunge into the swampy edges of the socialist quagmire over the past twenty-five years has come about, simply because the Kremlin, and the Kremlin's agents in this country, "planned it that way."

THE REAL SPUTNIK WAS LAUNCHED IN 1933 . . .

To change the metaphor, Comrade Khrushchev, the conspiratorial mechanism by which you are converting the United States into a communist country—to make it infinitely easier for you then to convert it into Communist satrapies ruled from Moscow—can be quite properly compared with a three-stage rocket. The first stage was fired in 1933, starting us with a "whoosh" on our way. Before the trajectory from that propulsion had leveled off we had already gone through: (1) the run on our banks and their resultant closing, in creating which hysteria your hands played the decisive unseen part, and which really supplied the launching stage for the whole rocket; (2) the establishment of the NRA, and the NLRB, and the boondoggling PWA, and the AAA, and all of the other alphabetical monstrosities of the New Deal—a great many of the leaders in which agencies have since been identified as active Communist agents or strong Communist sympathizers; (3) our joining the International Labor Organization, and the flooding into Washington from Montreal and Geneva of the agents of this strategy board of international socialism; (4) the placing over the heads of our formerly self-reliant people of the government umbrella of "social security"—largely through the influence and machinations of your ILO pals; (5) the Wagner Act, and a complete change in the direction, morals, and character of the American labor movement; (6) the introduction of class hatred into our country, which previously had hardly even been conscious of class lines; (7) a tremendous increase in the size, expensiveness, power, and reach of our federal bureaucracy; (8) an increasing subservience of both the legislative and judiciary branches of our government to the executive branch; (9) the gradual acceptance by the American people of the first significant use of the progressive principle of taxation; and (10) hundreds of other measures, large and small, designed by your Marxian predecessors to make the initial journey of any people into the boundaries of socialism appealing, deceptive—and irrevocable.

Was Refueled by the War . . .

The second stage of this rocket you managed, largely by conspiratorial diplomacy and aggressively lying propaganda in many countries, to get fired on December 7, 1941. And this second stage had the indescribably powerful propulsion given it by a worldwide war. Its trajectory has only now started to level off, after carrying us so much further into the socialist realm that we do not even need to recount here the milestones and markers which we have rushed past in mad flight. We do not believe any sensible man, whether he desires socialism or hates it, could deny that we are twice as far along in the direction you have wanted us to go as we were in 1941.

And Now Zooms Anew . . .

Then, in October 1957 your Sputnik set off the third stage of this far more important, though purely metaphorical, rocket. And once again, with a great "whoosh," we are on our way. The level of socialism to which you expect this rocket to carry us is simply astounding. We'll list, soon, many of the specific goals your agents have in mind, which will constitute and delineate that level. First we need to congratulate you, once more, on your cleverness.

For the propulsion and the "whoosh" of this third-stage projectile of your psychological rocket have not been provided altogether by your new kind of physical satellite. You and your fellow conspirators never do things by half, or leave any stone unturned which might conceivably make the success of your designs more certain. So, with the most beautiful timing imaginable, reports of the Gaither Committee, and of the study group of the Rockefeller Brothers Fund, and of assorted other committees and "study groups," have been following Sputnik and then each other with the precision of the hammer blows of a fancy clock striking the hour. And all of them have been driving into the American consciousness, as did Sputnik, the exact line of thought which you want lodged there at the present time. Like the confused general in the satirical epigram, the American nation is supposed to wake suddenly to a danger it does not understand, jump on its horse, and ride off in all directions at once. And under the present infiltrated leadership, it undoubtedly will.

WITH BOOSTERS . . .

We do not claim to know all of the details as to how you have accomplished this feat. But with more room to spare, Comrade Khrushchev, we believe we could play back for you a recognizable résumé of the most significant tactical steps. Suffice it to say here that the Gaither Committee seems to have been composed of the usual quota of innocents, opportunists, and some who are not so innocent at all. Among the "innocents" are men as devotedly patriotic as any in America, who are also among our country's most able businessmen. But their "innocence," once they get outside of their own bailiwick into the maze of politics and government, is ineffable. For the quickest illustration we can think of, these are the kind of men who insisted in 1952—and some of them even in 1956—that Eisenhower was a conservative Republican. In view of the record, even in 1952 entirely clear and readily available, that by his ideological convictions, his actions, and his associations, Eisenhower belonged in the left-wing fringes of the Democratic party, it would have been too much to expect of such men a realistic skepticism about any plausible-looking "facts" you arranged to have set before them.

Just how you managed, Comrade Khrushchev, even with all of your agents and dupes in our midst, to give the "facts" you wanted these men to get excited about all of the beguiling appearance of official "inside" information, and how many agents—if any—you had right inside the committee itself to help to steer the reaction to these "facts" in accordance with your wishes—is not important. It is the results that count.

AND SUPERCHARGERS . . .

As for the report of the Rockefeller Brothers Fund study group, the question as to how these men arrived at their conclusions does not even arise. For this report was nothing more nor less than a condensed rehash of a book already written by its chairman, Henry A. Kissinger. The book was swallowed from foreword to appendix without visible hesitation by the "study group," and presented anew to the public with the formality of a "report," and with the window dressing of "big names" to give it more attention. And since Professor Kissinger is a distinguished member of the Harvard faculty, there are certainly enough of your influences around him to push him pretty hard in the directions you desire.

At any rate, the tenor of both reports is exactly what you wanted to reinforce the psychological impact of Sputnik. And we learned long ago not to be blinded by studying the details of your pyrotechnic displays at too close hand. It is much more instructive, and gives a much more accurate understanding of what goes on, to stand off far enough to look at the pattern formed by these panoramic fireworks in their unified effect. In the present instance, as in many others, it is the superb synchronization that—next to the results themselves—most surely reveals your clever planning behind the separate displays which produce their composite magic.

ALL COMING IN ON CUE . . .

The Gaither Committee, the Rockefeller Brothers Fund study group, and other esoteric clusters now spouting the same extreme alarm—even to the hint that it might be wise to arm ourselves for a preventive war—have been gathering their "inside dope" for very varied periods. But at just the right time after your Sputnik was set up in the propaganda business, and at just the right time before our Congress got down to its job at this session, out came all of these reports to send shivers down our spine. It was all simply *too* pat, Comrade Khrushchev. Until your mathematical wizards (if any) succeed in amending the laws of probability, and in greatly lengthening the long arm of coincidence, we simply cannot buy such brilliant, deceptive concatenations, and their extremely important results, under the label of happenstance.

For added to these more definitive assaults on whatever clearheadedness we might still possess, there has mushroomed a great amorphous storm of similar propaganda. The way your whole worldwide machine is now clicking like clockwork, to bring every needed instrumentality and propaganda tool into play with just the right line at precisely the right time, is one of the most brilliant performances in your long experience with organized deception. And the objective of every stunt, every boast, every report, every line, and every voice is exactly the same: To frighten both us and our representatives into giving the American left wing everything even Karl Marx would ask for—all of it in the name of defense against Communist military might. The third stage of the rocket has been fired. From your point of view, it must not fail to carry the United States all of

the remaining way to socialism, finally so recognized and pro-
claimed; and every ounce of available strength of the Communist conspiracy must be marshalled—had to be marshalled—
at the exact time and place to give it all necessary propulsion.

V

Now that our rocket figure of speech has, we hope, served
its purpose of relating our forthcoming leftward movement to
similar glacial slides which began in 1933 and 1941—and in
calling attention to your planning and engineering behind all
three—let's abandon it. For in discussing specifically what the
Kremlin expects to accomplish through all of its currently concerted ballyhoo, we need to talk in plainer language.

Our first need is to point out that it *is* ballyhoo, not substance. At least ninety-five percent of all of America's sudden
fear of being destroyed or fatally injured by Russian weapons
of war is due to just the same old Communist bluff and bluster,
given a new injection of sound and fury. In the foreseeable
future, Comrade Khrushchev, you are *not* going to try to impose your tyranny on us, or on what would be left of us after
an all-out war, by launching any such war. For not only, in
our opinion and as already mentioned, do you lack the productive base to sustain a worldwide war now—even in comparison
with an enemy greatly weakened by whatever destruction you
could accomplish through surprise—but there are three other
controlling considerations.

You Also Have an "Enemy Within" . . .

The first of these is that the all-out worldwide war, to which
any direct attack on the United States by the Soviet Union
would certainly lead, would be the signal for a worldwide uprising of your enslaved subjects. For the desperately subdued
and separately powerless people in China, in Poland, in East
Germany, in every satellite and some "neutralist" dependencies,

even in Russia itself, would know that the time to fight for freedom was now or never. And your Communist core, ranging from perhaps one percent of the total population in China to five percent of that of Russia itself, simply would not be able, even with its brutal police state mechanics for holding the masses in control, to withstand any *simultaneous* uprising of all of your slaves and enemies—even with your tanks against their sticks and stones. Little wars, piecemeal conquests, "police actions," insurrections of natives against their "colonial" rulers, even isolated rebellions against yourself within your own domains; these disturbances you can afford to foment, and guide, and support or suppress, as the case may be, to have them best serve your ends. They are the sharp edge on the sword of your strategy. But the sword is not massive enough, and would not stay sharp long enough against such blunting resistance, to cover the planet with unfalteringly effective sweeps.

SIMPLER PLANS . . .

Second, you are looking forward to achieving your military formalization of your take-over of America, when the time does come, by having your side win the domestic *civil* wars which you will have instigated for that purpose—exactly as you have done in every other country where there was any real strength of opposition. And neither your fomenting of civil strife in America, nor even your hidden grasp of the reins of authority and communication, have yet gone far enough to make the stage ready for that performance.

And the third consideration is that you are winning the whole world now—and moving forward towards a final showdown *in*, not *with*, the United States—too rapidly and too surely, to be foolish enough to gamble your steadily materializing victory on an all-out test of military strength. We think you will keep right on working for that total victory by basically the same means that have been so successful for you in the past. And deception is the essence of your method.

And Surer Ways to Win . . .

For many years we Americans have been taken steadily down the road to Communism by steps supposedly designed, and presented to us, as ways of *fighting* Communism. Now, although the danger remains almost entirely *internal*, from Communist influences right in our midst and treason right in our government, the American people are being persuaded that our danger is from the *outside*, is from Russian military superiority. *Now* there is to be no limit to the plausible idiocy of the further steps to be taken under the excuse of matching this military strength, of preparing to defend ourselves from this threat of outside force. Our new secretary of defense has revealed the key to the overall program by announcing that "we may have to change our way of life." And you and your fellow Communists believe that you can stampede us into the biggest jump ever towards, and perhaps the final jump right into, socialism, communism, and then the Communist camp. Here are some of your obvious aims for the United States, to be achieved, you hope, through the momentum of the attitude induced by Sputnik and all of its auxiliary propaganda:

Specifically (For Us) . . .

(1) Greatly expanded government spending, for missiles, for so-called defense generally, for foreign aid, for every conceivable means of getting rid of ever larger sums of American money —as wastefully as possible.

(2) Higher taxes, and still higher taxes, and then much higher taxes.

(3) An increasingly unbalanced budget, despite the higher taxes.

(4) Increasing and ever more rapid inflation of our currency, leading in a parabolic curve to its ultimate worthlessness and complete repudiation.

(5) Government control of prices, wages, and materials, supposedly to combat inflation.

(6) Greatly expanded and intensified socialistic controls over every operation of our economy and every activity of our daily lives. This is to be accompanied, naturally and automatically, by a correspondingly huge increase in the size of our bureaucracy, and in both the cost and extensiveness of our domestic government.

(7) Far more centralization of power in Washington, especially in the executive branch of our government, and the gradual but practical elimination of our state lines.

(8) The steady advance of federal aid to, and control over, our educational system, leading to complete federalization of our public education.

(9) A constant pounding into the American mind of the horror of "modern warfare," and of the beauties and the absolute necessity of "peace"—peace, of course, always on Communist terms.

(10) And the consequent willingness of the American people to allow the steps of appeasement by our government which amount to a piecemeal surrender of the rest of the free world and of the United States itself to the Kremlin.

There is what Sputnik and all of its side decorations are really about. Those are the long-range results that we have to fear. If you and your fellow Communist conspirators can succeed in making us domestically a communist nation, it will not be too difficult a final move for you to pull us right into the worldwide Communist organization, ruled by Moscow. And unless we can have enough of a rebellion in our own country against the appeasement policies of our government *outside* and its communizing policies *inside* America, there isn't any doubt about your carrying out every one of the projected steps to your final goal, and reaching that goal itself.

VI

Of course, having Sputnik and Gaither and Kissinger running around, unconscious, in the orbits you have established for them, did not itself bring to pass any of the objectives outlined above. It merely provided the mental climate and the political opportunity for your agents and their sympathizers and dupes to initiate and carry through the practical measures leading to those objectives. Some few of these undertakings of your agents can be catalogued, much too briefly, as follows:

THE MECHANICS OF THE MOVEMENT . . .

(1) Continue to keep us alarmed over the danger of actual war.

(2) Increase the impression that the Communist party in the United States is rapidly declining in strength and numbers—while the number and power of your *secret* agents is growing by leaps and bounds.

(3) Carry through "Operation Abolition" to wipe out the congressional investigating committees and the FBI, or to render them helplessly ineffectual in exposing your agents and activities.

(4) Make Communism and Communists ever more respectable, and sedition itself merely a difference of opinion.

(5) Liquidate or smother all voices which would *tell the truth about your conspiracy*, and amplify those which sing the tunes you call.

(6) Have some of your most important secret agents in the United States attack Soviet Russia, and each other, at times and in ways to serve your careful plans. Confuse the people of this country concerning their leadership, and then double that confusion.

(7) Have conspicuous characters, who command public attention, skillfully delineate and pompously confess to so many shades of belief, from lightest pink to darkest red, all smoothly flowing into each other, that nobody will be courageous enough or clearheaded enough to draw a line and say: "On this side is merely 'liberalism,' but on this side is treason."

(8) Use the phony "civil rights" slogan to stir up bitterness and civil disorder, leading gradually to police state rule by federal troops and armed resistance to that rule.

(9) Break down our immigration barriers further, and smuggle more aliens in through what barriers do exist. (Mr. Richard Arens, our best-informed authority on the subject, states bluntly that there are now over three million aliens *illegally* in this country, a huge number of them under the control of your front the American Committee for Protection of Foreign Born.)

WITH PLENTY OF OIL . . .

(10) Promote more "cultural exchanges" between ourselves and Soviet Russia. This will provide more spies nosing openly into everything we do, while our visitors to Russia will be allowed to see only what you want them to see. It will further build up the impression that Communists are just like everybody else, only more so.

(11) Gather together ever new fronts of gullible innocents, controlled by a few of your secret agents, to rant publicly about everything from "peace" to repeal of the McCarran Act.

(12) Support vigorously, by every trick in the Communist political repertory, all legislation leading towards your major objectives.

(13) Flood the country with new "small" magazines of every description, each of them catering to the specialized area of interest of some segment of the American people, with no apparent room or reason for concern with the Communist issue— and each of them subtly promoting the Communist line as its real reason for existence.

TRANSMISSION BELTS . . .

(14) Organize an unending number of phony committees for "aid," or "information," or "liberation" of the people behind the Iron Curtain, so as to drain off money and energy of the American people that might otherwise go into honest anti-Communist causes.

(15) Push your own men ever further and higher in our

union labor organizations, and extend your power steadily over our whole labor movement. Not only does this give you a tremendous potential for sabotage in our economy whenever needed, but a "labor government" would be a most convenient first formal step in taking us over.

(16) See that our supposedly expanded, and certainly more expensive, missile program is kept in exactly those same hands which have so messed it up and delayed it—and allowed it to be sabotaged—before. You will need to keep pointing to our "lagging inferiority" in the most modern weapons, for many purposes.

(17) Promote ever more meetings, and ostentatious gestures of friendship, between members of your government and of ours. It increases despair and decreases resistance of anti-Communists on both sides of the Curtain.

(18) Get your known sympathizers elected ever more openly and brazenly to high positions in our great religious and educational organizations. It discourages opposition within those organizations as being hopeless and futile, and enables your agents to speak your lines with the *ostensible* support of millions behind them.

(19) Feed the prestige and power of the United Nations in every way possible. It's your baby—and has been ever since Alger Hiss served as midwife for its birth.

(20) Spread a belief in the inevitability and desirability of our recognition of Red China, and of its admission to the United Nations.

(21) Promote greater United States participation in ILO, WHO, and all similar international organizations. They dilute our sovereignty, our substance, and our anti-Communist determination.

AND WRENCHES . . .

(22) Stir up distrust and hatred between Jews and Gentiles, Catholics and Protestants, Negroes and whites, and all other

possible offsetting factions of our population, by every possible lie, smear, and distortion. Your first maxim for the conquest of any people is to divide them.

(23) Maintain and increase your working control over both of our major political parties. You do not have to fear that any firm and aggressive anti-Communist will be elected president, so long as you can keep one from being nominated.

(24) Expand the mental health racket just as rapidly as you can. Railroading your outspoken enemies into hospitals, as being "mentally sick," will become very useful long before you reach the police state ability to knock on a door at two o'clock in the morning and dispose of an enemy in such a way that he is never heard from again.

(25) Smear your effective enemies by every form of character assassination known. *After this has been accomplished,* or where it is insufficient, arrange "natural deaths," fatal "accidents," plausible "suicides," and—as a last resort—outright obvious murders, wherever getting rid of such an enemy seems worth the storm that may be raised. The only matter to be weighed in any case is the damage being done to your cause by the individual, against the extent to which your hand might be disclosed or surmised in his murder, and against the reaction of the public to the event.

This list, far from being exhaustive, is only a beginning. We could identify at least a hundred specific, similar efforts to which your agents in this country—open and secret, foreign and native—are assigned right now. But this is enough to serve our purpose—to let you know that we know what you are about. Most of these enterprises are exactly the same methods you have used in taking over other countries. Some are adjustments or extensions of your strategy, to cover the circumstances involved in annihilating the one greatest and final bastion of your opposition.

VII

We know, Comrade Khrushchev, that you and your associates take for granted that you will win—that it is only a matter of time. We know that most of the best-informed people on "our side" think the same thing. Most of my friends who have been in this fight the longest, and know the most about it, do not give us any chance whatever for survival. Some say we have one chance in a hundred, some one chance in fifty or thirty or twenty, as the case may be. Carl Byoir, who knew more about propaganda and its uses than any other American, stated before his death that we had "not more than" one chance in ten; and that is the most favorable probability I would be able to quote from anybody whose experience, judgment, and honesty in this field I respect.

Your Powerful Agents . . .

We know, Comrade Khrushchev, how deep, how far, and *how high* your infiltration has gone. Just a month ago a committee of the Massachusetts legislature officially cited thirty-seven more active Communists in this area, on top of twice that number named by it a few months before that. But these *identifiable* Communists are almost negligible in the total picture. What is much more important is that, within not too many miles from where we are writing these lines, there is a president of one institution of higher learning (not Harvard, incidentally), the president of one sizable bank, the dean of one law school, the editor of one newspaper, and the judge of one court whom we believe to be Communists; not merely ideological sympathizers with a communism which they foolishly mistake for humanitarianism, but active agents of an international conspiracy, subtly working for Communist conquest of the world. And our opinion, in every one of these cases, is shared by other students of your conspiracy who judge these men by the *ulti-*

mate results of what they do—which *always* help the Communists—rather than by the excuses they give for doing it. Yet every one of these men is a highly respected and—by the general public—utterly unsuspected member of the community.

YOUR INSTRUMENTALITIES OF THOUGHT CONTROL . . .

We know, Comrade Khrushchev, how unaware the American people are of the unseen tentacles of your conspiracy, now exerting their hidden pressures everywhere. To maintain this unawareness, you have employed on a tremendously larger scale the exact technique of opinion molding which Stalin used so successfully in Russia from 1924 to 1929. You have projected this technique into a system of influence and control over the media of mass communication in America that is probably the most gigantic accomplishment of its kind in human history. You have created a blanket of twisted information, misleading slants, subtle propaganda, and brazen falsehoods between the American people and any clear view of your activities. We admit that you have made every effort to pierce this blanket seem almost hopeless—and every light which is somehow thrust into the darkness seem pitiful in its candlepower. Not only do the American people as a whole have no idea of what is happening. Your propaganda machine has induced into them an unwillingness to believe the facts, no matter how incontrovertibly presented—or even to listen to the facts at all, so as to have any chance to believe.

YOUR IDEOLOGICAL SUBTERFUGE . . .

We know, Comrade Khrushchev, that too many influential Americans, in all good conscience, are blaming the visible results of your vast conspiratorial operations on "a worldwide spontaneous movement to the left, which nobody can do anything about." Just how *spontaneously* (!) this "movement to the left" has been welcomed is shown by the fact that the Peiping government has had to murder some forty million Chinese to keep itself in power and has—according to its own figures—had to suppress more than *five million* insurrections! Just how *spontaneous* was the "movement to the left," represented at a far different level and in different degree by the nomination of Eisenhower instead of Taft in 1952, is shown by the fact that the president of one of America's largest banks took suitcases full of currency to the convention to bribe delegates away from Taft; and that he was rewarded, for thus providing such *spontaneity*, by a major ambassadorship.

Five years ago the white people and the Negroes of our South, more peacefully inclined towards each other than at any time since the Civil War, were making tremendous progress in the solving of our difficult racial problem. But with the help of a huge book written by a Swedish collaborator of yours, of a Communist-contrived Supreme Court decision, of white Communists sent to serve as "secretaries" to notoriety-seeking Negro preachers, of a whole school for agitation run by Communists in Tennessee, and of ten thousand other acts and methods skillfully designed by your agents to stir up bitterness and riots, the whites and Negroes of the South are now giving dangerous vents to an increasing hatred—all, naturally, because of this *spontaneous* "movement to the left."

Of course the whole argument is camouflage for conspiracy, and the very words have been put into American minds and mouths by your agents. But even when we write a hundred pages of completely proved history to show that every detail of causation behind even some minor event was conspiratorial rather than ideological, the ordinary American replies: "Oh, but the Communists are not that clever. You give them too much credit." While in your mind, Comrade Khrushchev, the almost infinite amount of cunning and implementation, regularly meshed together by your organization, has always been justified by the prize at stake. We are fully conscious of the size of the job you have done in this country of hiding your hand and your cleverness in an all-pervasive fog of cleverness itself. We know from actual experience the frustrating near-impossibility of dispelling that fog at any point for any moment—and how quickly it closes in again. We do not underrate any of the advantages which you hold.

AND YOUR LOATHSOME TACTICS . . .

Finally, we know we cannot fight you with your kind of weapons. For you and your agents are prepared to use—will delight in using—every foulness which you have tried so successfully in the past in order to accomplish your purposes. A pragmatic amorality—the lack of any belief in moral absolutes, or any conception of good or bad—is a fundamental philosophic principle of your following. While we, fighting to save our civilization as well as our lives, must confine ourselves to civilized means and methods. We not only believe that there are other ends to an individual's life than the pursuit of personal power and the conversion of humankind into a soulless serfdom to the state. We believe that even the means used by each of us separately, and all of us collectively, to achieve those various ends, however noble—or even to defend ourselves—must conform to basic ideas of right or wrong. These concepts have evolved over thousands of years as common factors in all of our great religions. You and your fellow barbarians of the Kremlin, as well as those suave savages who work for you in America, are counting on the handicaps imposed on us by the very things we are fighting for to help you and them to destroy us.

DO NOT FRIGHTEN US ENOUGH . . .

We know all of these things, Comrade Khrushchev, and a great many other reasons for discouragement. Yet—and this, at last, is the whole point of our letter—we do not share the defeatism of our learned friends. Maybe that is why; we are not scholarly enough to accept any verdict in advance; or—in a more vernacular expression—to know when we are licked. For we do know that history is full of apparently lost causes that still emerged victorious. We simply refuse to be licked; and for that reason, among others, we do not think that we shall be.

WHILE YOU TREMBLE AT YOUR RISK . . .

For we have one all-powerful weapon, Comrade Khrushchev, and our only need is to get it unsheathed. That weapon is the truth. To unsheathe it we must make the American people understand what is really taking place, and how, and why—and we must do this before it is too late. This—simply having the American people realize the truth—is the only thing in all the world today that you and your cohorts fear. But because of your fear of this one possibility, you still live, behind your ghoulish grins, in a constant state of sweat and strain and terror. As well you should.

BUT THERE IS ONE WAY OUT . . .

This may sound like ants challenging an elephant. But elephants have been killed by ants in the past, and the wise elephant does not get himself hopelessly entangled in an angry swarm. This warning is the fundamental justification for this letter. There is one, and only one, possible course which might extricate both you and us from the impasse to which your conspiratorial schemes have now brought us all. This is, simply give up and *call off* your conspiracy. Put all of your energy and cleverness into raising the mental and physical living standards of the Russian people. Everything in the whole worldwide horror and turmoil you have caused can then be handled and eventually straightened out within the framework of civilized human relationships. And you will become a man who really changed the course of history in a happier direction, instead of merely a nasty blot on one of its gloomiest pages.

VIII

We do not expect you to heed this advice, Comrade Khrushchev, so we shall not belabor the argument. Having made this "positive" approach for the sake of fairness and however little consideration you might give it, we continue with a "negative" warning which you are better able to understand. There are now many thousands of us in America—of whom this writer is only one unimportant example—who have given up careers, incomes, possessions, all hopes of personal peace and leisure, and their whole lives to the one task of alerting as many of our fellow citizens as we can to the methods and the menace of the Communist conspiracy. Our numbers, our strength, and our experience are growing together. We have leaders who are now veterans in this fight—Fulton Lewis, Clarence Manion, Dan Smoot, Bonner Fellers, Frank Kirkpatrick, Frank Hanighen, and a hundred more I could name—and who, despite your vicious efforts to smother them, are increasing their total influence every week. And at least the progress of your conspiracy, though not its methods, becomes daily easier to demonstrate to those we can persuade to listen.

WE FIND ENCOURAGEMENT, TOO . . .

We are denied the use of most of the newspapers, magazines, television programs, radio programs, and even book-publishing channels which already have large established audiences—by your binding influence exerted in ways too numerous, too subtle, and too powerful for us to delineate them here. But we are finding ways to run your blockade, and to reach with print or voice a still small but increasing percentage of the people of this country. Also, we are helped mightily by one intangible aid—the intuition of our "grass-roots" neighbors. For while the American people do not know what is wrong, nor have any idea how badly it is wrong, they sense that something *is* wrong. Despite all of the specious explanations given them to account for our steady loss of ground, they are vaguely but deeply disturbed. And with the new converts we are gaining daily, who in turn become crusaders for this same enlightenment, our new enrollments are going to increase faster than you can smear us out of effectiveness, or silence us by murder.

Just suppose, Comrade Khrushchev—and shudder at the possibility—that this very letter were placed in the hands of, and read by, only one million Americans. It might set off a chain reaction of truth-seeking which would rip your whole blanket of lies and subtle censorship into shreds—something you fear infinitely more than all of our hydrogen bombs and NATO alliances. It won't happen. Your silencers are too well entrenched for that. Full many an effort like this, each one reaching its comparatively few thousands, will have to be sweated out by many minds, before we blast any decisive holes in that entrenchment. We know that the momentum of your spreading, descending power in America is tremendous. It is far greater than any offsetting resistance we can hope to create in the near future. But the resistance which we do seed wherever we can is now taking root, and growing, and bearing the fruit of more resistance in many fertile plots. We recognize the Herculean task that we face. But we assure you, and warn you, that we shall not give up the fight as long as we breathe; that for each of us who goes down, two will arise to replace him; and that—knowing what you hope most—we shall not despair.

IN KNOWLEDGE OF THE PAST . . .

For, contrary to another of your vaunted lies, Comrade Khrushchev, history (or human experience) is clearly on our side. Your British socialist allies know this, if you do not. It is why they felt obliged to subsidize a hack named Toynbee to rewrite history the way they wanted it to appear. For socialism is merely a degenerative disease in a body politic which will have to be excised out of even your own country before you can ever become really strong in anything but bluff and cunning, or can rule by any means except cruelty and deception. Conspiracies, no matter how successful for a while, do not last. And human beings simply will not stay enslaved.

AND IN OUR OWN DETERMINATION . . .

The question is not whether your gang will be destroyed, but when; how much farther you can still go before you will be stopped and routed. Your planning is terrific, your patience superb, and your ambition is truly epic. You may actually reach, for a precarious moment, a position of world rulership, with even the United States held formally and temporarily in thrall. But if so, your empire will be blown to bits almost immediately by the forces within it, as was that of Sparta shortly after it conquered—by the same kind of infiltration and treason —Athens and the whole Greek world. And it was Athens, not Sparta, that lasted and contributed to the current of civilization.

Our goal is to see that you do not even get that far, and there are plenty of us willing to die in the effort. We do not relish sounding melodramatic, Comrade Khrushchev, for melodrama *should be* out of place in the expression of such sober thoughts. But you have, by the studied theatricality of your incessant maneuvers, deliberately made melodrama the very mood of contemporary existence. So we cannot speak our lines with any effectiveness without climbing onto the same stage where you strut. With embarrassment, but simple earnestness, therefore, let us repeat: There are plenty of us willing to give our lives, whenever necessary, in this battle. All we ask is to make those lives cost you enough. And some of us have given much more thought to that bargain than did Taft, or McCarthy, or many of your lesser victims such as we would be.

Only a few months ago a close personal friend of this writer, who had bought and distributed several thousand dollars worth of our books, was—in our considered opinion—murdered in cold blood by your agents, because he was distributing tens of thousands of dollars worth of other anti-Communist literature also. And so unwilling were our pusillanimous metropolitan press and hamstrung law enforcement agencies to stir up your powerful secret antagonism, that they gladly let this murder ride as an utterly fantastic suicide—just as they did the equally fantastic and unbelievable "suicide" of James Forrestal. But this victim of your "preventive measures" made one mistake. He had not made careful plans as to how his untimely death—from any cause—would create more disturbance in your smooth-running plans than the damage caused you by what he was doing. Some of us will try to do better.

Our "Ancient Founts of Inspiration" . . .

As for any sneer on your part that this expressed willingness to give life itself for our cause is out-Khrushchev-ing Khrushchev in histrionics, let me try to disillusion you. Nearly two years ago we quoted in this magazine, with premeditated purport, Macaulay's famous lines that now seem to the oversophisticated so much out of date:

> And how can man die better
> Than facing fearful odds
> For the ashes of his fathers
> And the temples of his Gods.

You should get one of your more trusted agents, Comrade Khrushchev, to make a survey of just how often those lines have appeared since, in various little "right-wing" publications throughout the United States. And if your agent is an expert in psychology, he might discover and reveal to you just how accurately those lines express the silent reflections of the men and women who reprinted them. And of many a reader, too. We all must die sometime. And so we ask ourselves, in simple sincerity, just how *can* man die better—especially if in doing so he appreciably reduces the odds against his compatriots in the fight. "Is life so dear, or peace so sweet, as to be purchased at the price of chains and slavery?" We know that you have been personally responsible, Comrade Khrushchev, for the planned and deliberate murder of literally millions of your fellow human beings. (See *Reader's Digest,* September 1957.) So we know you are not playing. We want you also to know that neither are we.

You boast that you will bury us, and that our grandchildren will live under socialism. Maybe so, Comrade, but we do not believe it. As for your cunning attempt, even in that boast, to deceive us into considering remote a danger which is indeed very close, we see through that, too. There is far more likelihood that we, of the present generation, will live for a while—those of us who do live—under your gang's dominion, than that our grandchildren will. For freedom will have been restored by then, at whatever cost.

Your Lack of Any Support of the Spirit . . .

The ultimate reason, however, Comrade Khrushchev, for our confidence that in the long run it is we who shall bury your conspiracy—instead of your burying us—lies in the difference in what we are fighting for. You cannot base a "way of life" on the cruelty, repression, exploitation, lies, deception, amorality, and eternal scheming and jockeying for personal power of a ruling class that constitutes less than five percent of a population, and then expect loyalty to that "way of life" and to that ruling class on the part of the regimented and oppressed serfs when the showdown comes. Just where, Comrade Khrushchev, do you find the men who are willing to die to defend the lies and cruelty—to themselves—of their masters? Remember Kiev. You had been the absolute autocrat of the Ukraine for twelve years when you made your impassioned speech that your capital city defend itself valiantly against the oncoming German armies. The outstanding feature in the destructive advance of those armies so far had been the stampede of your soldiers and subjects to surrender. Four days after your speech, the city of Kiev proper followed suit without firing a shot.

With so large a proportion of your own subjects your bitterest enemies, as is shown by your constant concern with possible insurrection, how can you expect them to become your loyal supporters for the purpose of enslaving others? Even the millions wearing uniforms in your armed forces, and subject to all the brutal discipline and indoctrination of your "democratic" army, could not be trusted for a minute. Remember how, near the end of World War II, one detachment after another of your troops, even while breathing victory in their nostrils, surrendered enthusiastically to General Vlasov's army in German uniform—just as soon as they discovered that this army was led by a Russian bent on liberating Russia from your rule? Or remember that, even in suppressing the Hungarian Revolt, you did not dare trust your European soldiers, but sent tanks armed by Mongolians, who had no understanding of why they were fighting, or of whom. Of what avail your missiles or your submarines or planes, if those who man them have nothing to die for, when the time comes to use these weapons in war against your enemies?

AND OUR LOYALTIES THAT GO BEYOND PATRIOTISM . . .

We, it is true, are complacent with prosperity, justly distrustful of much of our leadership, divided among ourselves, and now greatly lacking in the moral stamina and fearless patriotism of our fathers. But we have an inheritance of freedom and a traditional "way of life," which we have ourselves enjoyed, and which a vast majority of us feel is worth any sacrifice to maintain for our descendants. While many of us consciously, and most of us unconsciously, have a motivation, Comrade Khrushchev, which goes even deeper. It is a loyalty to the best in human nature, to the ideals of truth and justice and compassion and individual integrity, which man has slowly and haltingly acquired over thousands of years. We do not believe that the toil and teaching through the ages of the saints and the philosophers, the fighters and the poets, the workers and the dreamers, who have created such civilization as we now have, are to be cast aside as useless and in vain. We may blindly lose our gratitude, our perspective, and our vision for the future during absorption in the little games that constitute our daily lives. But underneath all of this apparent callousness, we have a pride in what has been created for us by the noblest minds and soundest builders among those who have gone before. And the most important element in all of this inheritance, material or spiritual—formed by the contributions of millions of men, each trying to be more worthy of the life given him by whatever concept of the Divine he worshipped—*is the composite human conscience.*

WILL BRING THE WORLD ANOTHER MORNING AFTER THIS DARK NIGHT . . .

This amorphous but quite palpable total human conscience, Comrade Khrushchev, you and your power-hungry fellow conspirators against civilization would utterly spurn and destroy. But we are sure that, instead, its influence will bring about your own destruction. For we "doubt not through the ages one increasing purpose runs." *And that eternal purpose is not cruelty, lies, and tyranny, but kindness, truth, and freedom.* It is against the power of that unswerving long-range purpose that your foul and degrading conspiracy will break to pieces. And better men of a better age will wonder how their ancestors could have tolerated, and been frightened by, such beasts as you and your fellow criminals—for even so brief a moment in the life story of the human race.

—ROBERT WELCH

OZYMANDIAS OF EGYPT

I met a traveller from an antique land
Who said: Two vast and trunkless legs of stone
Stand in the desert . . . Near them, on the sand,
Half sunk, a shattered visage lies, whose frown,

And wrinkled lip, and sneer of cold command,
Tell that its sculptor well those passions read
Which yet survive, stamped on these lifeless things,
The hand that mocked them, and the heart that fed:
And on the pedestal these words appear:
"My name is Ozymandias, king of kings:
Look on my works, ye Mighty, and despair!"
Nothing beside remains. Round the decay
Of that colossal wreck, boundless and bare,
The lone and level sands stretch far away.

—Percy Bysshe Shelley

Through All the Days to Be

As first delivered in the Shrine Auditorium in Los Angeles on April 11, 1961. The subheads have been added for the printed version.

IT IS MY UNDERSTANDING that there is a division of labor here tonight. My job is to talk, yours is to listen. But if you get through before I do, will you please let me know. And so that we may know where we stand, will all Communists in the audience please hold up their right hands.

When I first began speaking in public I was told that the size of any audience always reflected simply how good the last speaker before that same group had been. So, looking at this audience, I have decided that my good friend Tom Anderson, who spoke to the Freedom Club last week, is an even more outstanding orator than I had thought him to be, and that was already very outstanding indeed. My only regret is over what I'm going to do tonight to another good friend of mine, Dr. Orval Watts, your speaker for next week. Orval may have to promise trading stamps to get anybody to come to hear him.

REASONS TO LISTEN . . .

Seriously, and actually, the number of you good citizens who have been kind enough to come out to hear me tonight is a reflection of something far more important than the quality of your speakers, past, present, or future. You are deeply concerned, of course, over many things. One is the gradual but visible loss of the independence and sovereignty of the United States to an international socialist government. Another is the equally gradual and visible conversion of that potential one-world government, right while it is in the making, into the worldwide police state of brutal Communist tyranny for which the socialist supergovernment is only a forerunner and a front. One is the obvious speed and ruthlessness with which the Communist iron fist within the socialist velvet glove is now pounding to pieces all remaining resistance in so many countries of the world, and making the ultimate total conquest of the whole planet by the Communists appear not only inevitable but imminent. You have good reason to be worried, not only about the prospect of your grandchildren living in a socialist world, as Khrushchev promised, but of yourselves living in a slave state under brutal Communist masters, and in just a few more years.

In the fall of 1958, when The John Birch Society was founded, I pointed out to the handful of great Americans who attended the original two-day meeting that in my opinion the method was quite clear on which the Communists were relying most heavily in their plans to take us over.

Our subjugation was to be accomplished by a process so gradual and insidious that Communist rule would be slipped over so far on the American people before they ever realized it was happening that patriots would no longer be in control of the government, resisting the efforts of Communists to overthrow that government. Instead, without the change, or the decisive steps in the change ever having been visible, the Communists would be in control of government, and patriotic Americans could resist the further consolidation and extension of officially clothed Communist power only by themselves becoming conspirators against the established government. And I further said that in my opinion, even then in 1958, the process in that direction was already going on, gradually but surely and with ever-increasing certainty and speed. Today the process has gone so far that not only our federal government but some of our state governments are to a disturbing extent controlled by Communist sympathizers or political captives of the Communists. Many of our national organizations and groupings of our people are visibly and disturbingly subject to Communist influences in the top echelons of control. And the use of typical Communist riot and terror tactics has already gone all the way from the breaking up of the hearings of the HCUA in San Francisco last year to the brutal physical attack on a patriotic young man, simply for writing anti-Communist material for his paper, right here in Los Angeles last month. And you say to yourselves: "Just what on earth does it take to make the American people recognize the Communist steamroller at work?" So you worry about seeing our own country soon become just another group of provinces in a Communist empire.

AND TO WORRY . . .

And you would think all of that would be worry enough. But there is more—much, much more. For the more thoughtful among you realize that our whole civilization is at stake and in serious danger. All of the humanizing customs and traditions and tolerance of the views and wishes of others, which man has so laboriously achieved, are being wiped out by the Communists through the means they use to acquire and maintain power.

Castro was glorified, even in the American press, because his guerillas fought their way to power in Cuba without wearing uniforms. There was no way the poor farmers in Oriente Province could distinguish friend from foe, or the men who were out to burn their homes and murder their families from neighbors seeking to protect both. This fighting of a war, and especially a civil war, without distinctive uniforms is a barbarism man had outgrown a thousand years ago, until the Communists adopted it as a standard technique of their terror.

Even in the brutalities and crimes and wars man had by no

means been able to eliminate from the lives of his most enlightened generations, certain softening rules and customs had become so widely accepted and observed as to make possible an increasingly civilized and humanitarian existence. Until the Communists came along, wars had to be *declared*, and certain provisions followed for enabling friends and foes to get on their respective sides. Now the Communists depend on the very fact of not declaring war as one of their greatest assets in waging one. Until the Communists came along, solemnly established treaties were expected by even the most cynical students of geopolitics, to be intended as settlements of lasting duration of various conflicts, disagreements, or common purposes—whether the intentions held very long or not. But the Communists brazenly proclaim that treaties, like pie crusts, are made to be broken. And they are frequently making plans as to when and how to break any treaty most advantageously for themselves right while the treaty is being formulated.

The impact of the Communists has been the same on all of the arts of peace as well as the arts of war. Pictures are not painted for their beauty, nor music composed for its addition of harmony to life, nor books written for the increase of man's knowledge or enjoyment, but all art must be prostituted to the service of the Communist conspiracy and to the lust for power of the top conspirators.

In my opinion one of the most ennobling as well as most pleasing of all man's arts is great poetry. And as those here who are most familiar with the Blue Book of The John Birch Society know, I tried to put what the advance of Communism was doing and would do to all of the arts in general, and to poetry in particular, in a sonnet written to my good friend Alfred Noyes a few months before he died. To those who abhor an Alexandrine as the last line of a sonnet, I plead *nolo contendere*. To those who already have heard the sonnet too many times before, I apologize. But I should like to read it to all others in this audience anyway, because it summarizes, as concisely as I know how, what is happening to our whole civilization.

To Alfred Noyes

As after Rome, now once again the drapes
　　Of ignorance and bigotry and lust
　　May close upon the scene. Insentient dust
Will bury the forgotten stage. And apes
Who know not man, his glory and his dreams,
　　His wish to be more worthy of his God,
　　Will stalk the earth and wield the brutal rod,
And stamp upon each tiny light that gleams.
Amid the dull collective monotone
　　Of universal serfdom will be lost
The memory of song and singer. Prone
　　And helpless, soon, upon the rubbish tossed,
Will die the Muse. Let us rejoice to own
　　This one great poet more before the holocaust.

If the murder of the muses goes far enough; if the regimentation and subordination of the sciences to the purely pragmatic purposes of the Communists becomes complete enough; if the level of man's capacity through free market interchange to produce and distribute the material needs of life is reduced low enough by the chaos of socialist planning; and if the opportunity and incentive for individuals to contribute infinitely varied trial-and-error undertakings to our whole social and economic system is destroyed completely enough by Communist police state regimentation; if these tragic developments are consummated before the Communists are stopped, then even when the whole brutal tyranny is eventually broken and scattered to the winds of piecemeal revolt, the irreparable damage to our civilization will already have been done. The only possible environment for human life will be a new and feudal Dark Ages out of which man once more will have to emerge slowly and painfully—recovering over centuries the arts and sciences and skills and freedoms and total attributes of the civilization we have, just as our ancestors recovered over centuries the Greek and Roman inheritance which had been so largely lost. And to those of us who wish to transmit to our children and their children as much as possible of both the glorious country and humane civilization which we ourselves inherited, this whole imminent prospect is a cause of deep and unceasing anxiety. For we, the heirs of all ages, are simply abandoning, rather than improving, our marvelous inheritance.

II

But even this is not the ultimate or most important worry. To those in this audience and other groups throughout the country who are most aware of what the Communists are really doing, and how they are doing it, there is a tragic possibility far more significant even than those already outlined, and about which we need to be even more profoundly concerned. For you may have observed that in listing above the losses and dangers that now face us, I had not yet come to any question of religion or morality, nor to one of the basic problems with which The John Birch Society is so vitally concerned. This problem is not simply the increasing lack of morality in all human conduct, nor the corresponding immorality because of weakening consciences, but something far more disastrous, which we have described as the flight to amorality. And I wanted to approach this subject as part of a more inclusive one. For what we are really facing today, Ladies and Gentlemen, is an effort so sinister, so extensive, and so far-reaching with regard to man's future, that it can only be described as diabolical, in the most literal and frightening meaning of that word.

REACHING FAR INTO THE FUTURE . . .

In this audience there are plenty of good and great men and women who believe in a personal, living devil, devoting his eternal cunning and hatred to destroying God's hopes for man. There are others, still devoutly religious, who think of the same struggle in more impersonal images, as an eternal battle between light and darkness, truth and falsehood, right and wrong, or good and evil. They simply leave unresolved for others, and perhaps unresolved even for themselves, some of the questions as to the form and nature of the Deity they worship as the source of all being in the world man knows; and as the Creator of the environment, the forces, the human aspirations, and the incredible gift of free will, which together constitute the framework within which men live and seek ever to "rise on stepping stones of their dead selves to higher things." And among you there are all shades of specific belief in between. But the great common denominator of all these beliefs is that all of you—or almost all—see and know and feel that there are forces of evil battling with the forces of good, within each individual and within the whole human race, for the ultimate fate of all mankind.

Now always before, all but the tiniest insignificant fraction of mankind has at least paid lip service to the morality which seemed to a particular age to be in tune with an "upward reach" given by God to man. Nobody claimed that the recognized virtues were not to be honored, or that the slowly evolving moral sense of man was not desirable and important. Even Machiavelli would have considered excellent morals in his prince as a most desirable and appealing personal luxury if the prince could afford them. We have had crime and sin and falsehood before on a large scale and throughout all ages, but never before as the accepted customs and honored characteristics of a worldwide cult. They were, in all previous eras, regarded as trespasses against religion or society or both. Individuals committing heinous crimes, to obtain a throne or to destroy an enemy, might still be honored by a majority of their fellowmen; but it was despite or in disregard of their sins, not because of those sins. Their crimes against God and their fellowmen were not the visible and admitted reasons for the honors bestowed on them, or for the responsibilities and power committed to their hands.

Now, for the first time in all history on any extensive scale —let alone on any worldwide scale—we have the forces of evil openly and brazenly setting up their precepts and values and codes as the acceptable and preferable *mores* of mankind. We see a conscious, deep-rooted, long-range, deliberate, incredibly determined and diabolically cunning attempt to have the evil in man's nature become revered instead of the good; to have man's God-given "upward reach" replaced by a Satanically cruel "downward reach"; and to reverse the whole course of man's ages-long and often painful self-education in the nature of spiritual values. What is really at stake today, overshadowing all lesser gains and losses, is the very nature of human life and the very purpose of man *through all the days to be*.

That is what I wish primarily to talk to you about tonight. And if any of you feel any slightest disappointment at the prospect that I may not be talking about Communism and the Communist menace, don't. For I shall be talking almost entirely about Communism. And it is my hope to give you an insight into the whole basic strategy of the Communist drive, as well as into a basic ultimate aim of those who would establish Communism as a religion, supplanting all other religions, which— as it seems to me—has not been sufficiently realized by most of those opposing the Communists nor even by a majority of the opportunistic Communist millions doing the bidding of their masters.

III

The concept involved I have called, for lack of a better phrase, the Principle of Reversal. And it is the comprehensiveness of the application of that principle, and not simply that it is used, which is so surprising. It is the fact, gradually unfolding to the student, that the Principle of Reversal is not just a part or an element of Communist strategy, but *is* Communist strategy, that becomes so startling and so important.

In Semantics . . .

Let's first make clear what we are talking about in the easiest and surest way, by the use of illustrations. And the field of semantics is the best area in which to look for illustrations that are already recognized by most informed anti-Communists. By the "liberation" of a country for instance, such as Cuba, the Communists mean the imposing on Cuba of a tyrannical Communist dictatorship. And they do not consider that "liberation" complete until the viceroy of the Kremlin is so safely established that all resistance seems futile to the enslaved people under him.

Or let's look at the much overworked Communist phrase "anti-colonialism." It was invented by the Communists in about 1920. Or at least it was first put into use by them in that year by their agitators on the Pacific Coast of Asia, from Korea all the way down China and Indochina to Malaysia, Singapore, and Indonesia. At that time, and since then, right up through all of the troubles created so far by the Communists in Africa, the term has been used as a slogan and a weapon to drive out of one "underdeveloped" country after another the civilizing influences and stabilizing governments of the British, Dutch, French, and other leading powers. Its avowed purport has been to rid Asia and Africa of "colonialism" and the supposedly corresponding exploitation of native populations by European nations, and thus to make those nations free and independent. Its real purpose at all times has been exactly the opposite, and that was to supplant the beneficent and generally helpful colonialism of the civilized western European nations—and of the United States as in the Philippines—with the infinitely more oppressive, harsh, exploitative and tyrannical "colonialism" of the Russia-centered worldwide Communist dominion. The Soviet empire has gone on busily and successfully establishing itself as the greatest and also the most tyrannical "colonial" power of all time quite effectively and very largely by its unending and always bitter campaign against "colonialism."

There are dozens of other important examples of this reversal of the meaning of words and phrases. George Orwell's great book *1984* is largely based on the "doubletalk" and "doublethink" which such words represent. But this is sufficient to make the basic principle clear. And more illustrations will come out anyway in the course of our look at other uses of the whole Principle of Reversal. So let's go now to the application of that principle, which has been devastatingly successful in forwarding Communist purposes, especially in the United States.

In Our Foreign Aid Program . . .

For years we have been taken steadily down the road to Communism by steps supposedly designed, and presented to the American people, as ways of *fighting* Communism. The whole foreign aid program is an excellent example. Our foreign aid program has done some good, of course. The Communists, being intensely practical and realistic, even in their most cunning stratagems, do not believe in using solid black instrumentalities, but dark gray ones. They are always willing to be hurt, or to take losses here and there, for the sake of an ultimate net gain in any transaction or endeavor. And American foreign aid, from the time it began as a contribution of some seventy-two percent of UNRRA funds, until it has reached the mammoth proportions of today, has been a tremendous help to the advance of Communism.

It was planned by the Communists for that purpose. This pouring of American billions into foreign countries, to make things easier for the Communists and their socialist allies or agents, is exactly what the Communists wanted the American government to do. Our UNRRA funds were used by Menshikov in Poland and by Madame Sun Yat-sen's associates in China as powerful weapons to reward the natives who would join the Communists and to beat down through starvation the natives who were willing to resist. Our billions in money and materials delivered to Tito were used as completely to strengthen the international Communist conspiracy as if they had been delivered directly to the Kremlin. Our money and guns delivered to Sukarno in Indonesia were at times for the specific purpose of enabling him to put down anti-Communist revolts of the Indonesian army units and people. And the recent, even more brazen deliveries of American wealth to Communists like Gomulka in Poland show how far this whole Big Lie called foreign aid can be carried once the Big Lie has been repeated and acted on long enough.

IN OUR DEFENSE OUTLAY . . .

Another excellent example of the same strategy at work has been the impact of the Soviet military threat on our domestic economy. The Soviets never were able to conquer *Finland* by their own military force. They didn't take over even tiny Albania, or Poland, or Cuba, or Bolivia by direct use of Soviet arms, but always by internal subversion which was carried to the point of civil war only if necessary. What on earth leads anybody to think that the Soviets, in view of their whole past history, would attempt to conquer their most powerful enemy by military force when they are doing it so easily, rapidly, and successfully by internal subversion? Especially when you consider that an all-out shooting war between the Soviets and ourselves would be the automatic signal, the now-or-never trumpet call, for the *simultaneous* uprising of the enslaved peoples all over the world, which is the only development of a military nature that the Kremlin really fears.

Although our danger remains almost entirely internal from Communist influences right in our midst and treason right in our government, the American people have been persuaded exactly the opposite—that our danger was from the outside, from Soviet military might. And so, under the excuse of preparing to match that military might, of defending ourselves from this threat of outside force—in other words, under the guise of fighting Communism—we have been stampeded and are still being stampeded into taking more and more of those measures which convert us into a socialist state. The long-range object is: So to change the economic and political structure of the United States that it can be comfortably merged with Soviet Russia in a one-world socialist government.

From a military point of view the Soviets proceed against the United States on the soundest of strategy. It calls for paralyzing their enemy and their enemy's will to resist by internal subversion before ever striking a blow. Not until the Soviets have complete victory already assured is there any slightest danger of the use of Soviet arms or armies on American soil. If and when it does come it will be merely part of a "mopping up" operation to destroy potential resistance movements within America by mass murder and limitless terror. To the hopeless slaves of the Communist tyranny elsewhere in the world this would be no signal for revolt but clear evidence that the Soviets were merely suppressing revolt, or preventing future revolt, by their usual methods, in another territory that had already been conquered.

It is precisely because no earthly power could drag the Soviets into a real war or an honest war with the United States today that they beat their breasts so much and threaten war so loudly and so often. I believe that, just as a matter of sound common sense and of permanent national policy, we should keep our powder dry—and keep plenty of it. But we should also remain constantly and acutely aware of the incredible waste of billions of dollars, the socialization of our economy, the centralization of government power, and all of the other Soviet-serving measures being so skillfully promoted by Communist influences within our government, with this completely phony threat of outside war as the excuse.

IV

But our concern in this speech is with the Principle of Reversal, and we should not let our illustrations lead us too far into the specific matters with which they deal. So let's look into another area where the Communists have had the principle busily at work for a long time. And this is in the manufacture of slogans for what I have described elsewhere as their continuing campaign of "conquest by catchphrase."

IN SLOGANS . . .

Any serious and objective student of the history of the past quarter of a century will already have discovered the Communist planning and promotion behind most of these slogans, no matter how cleverly and how extensively the Communist themselves were able to stay behind the scenes, and to beguile perfectly innocent leaders in American political life (and often in other fields as well) to spread such effective propaganda for them. But even to those patriotic Americans who have not yet run into the more direct and substantive evidence of the Communist origin and propagation of these epigrammatic weapons, the remarkable similarity in their construction and pattern is enough to carry conviction as to their common source. When you then note, from the advantages of long hindsight, how invariably and extensively such slogans have helped the Communist cause, no matter how little this was realized at the time by the very people most ambitiously spreading the slogans, the realization becomes inescapable that the catchphrases represented brilliant Communist psychological warfare at work. Then and only then it is time to note that the Principle of Reversal was involved every time.

In 1940 the most important thing in the world to Stalin was to get the United States into the war. For several years his secret agents and his diplomatic agents in Japan, in England, in the United States, and in dozens of other places had been scheming and lying and conniving to bring on World War II for the advantages of making the Soviets a wartime ally of the western nations, and for the sake of the sociological changes and the chaos and the resulting opportunities for the Communists which the war and its aftermath would provide.

And by 1940 President Franklin D. Roosevelt had made it amply clear that, if he could win a third term and stay in power, he would bring the United States into the war as soon as he could manage it. The problem, however, was that Roosevelt had to be reelected first. And not only did he have to overcome the objection to a third term, but he had to overcome something far more deep-rooted, solid, and extensive. That was the opposition of a vast majority of the American people to his *foreign policy*, which was visibly heading us into a war of which the ordinary American citizen wanted no part.

I CAN'T STAND ROOSEVELT, BUT . . .

Of course by 1940 Roosevelt's whole New Deal had been shown to be foreign, phony, and a failure. And his demagoguery was already recognized by millions who had voted for him with such docile gullibility in 1936. But demagoguery with regard to domestic issues has never been much of a flaw in the political appeal of American candidates for office. And if the millions repelled by it can be counterbalanced by other millions whose votes are bought with the tax money provided by that demagoguery, the demagogue has little cause to worry on that particular score. The feeling against our getting involved in another world war, however, had a depth and extensiveness that could not be brushed aside or bowled over by the usual political ballyhoo. More desperate and more brilliant steps were required. And it is just one of many such steps taken which concerns us here. That was the creation, dissemination, and ultimate spreading all over the United States, until it became almost a byword, of the catchphrase: "I can't stand Roosevelt, but we *must* support him because of his foreign policy."

Now there are several principles of Communist psychological warfare at work here. One, which we have already seen in connection with our foreign aid program, is "Always give up something for the sake of a greater gain." By conceding something unfavorable about Roosevelt in the remark; by having the very conservatives in domestic affairs at whom this whole campaign was aimed, and who innocently picked up this slogan and parroted it to their friends, voice their basic dislike for Roosevelt, which would be shared by their listeners; by this gambit the slogan would be—and was—tremendously more convincing in the second part, which was what the Communists wanted to put over. It is a trick which the Communist propaganda machine uses over and over in variations to fit a lot of different needs. The pattern grows out of, or is related to, a fundamental precept of dialectical materialism: "Take two short steps backward for each long step forward." Whether both short steps come before or after the one long step, or one before and one after, doesn't matter, so long as the one forward step exceeds in distance the sum of the two backward ones.

But the trick in the slogan under observation which really concerns us here is the Communists' habit of taking their greatest weakness and, by daring and bluff, converting it into their greatest item of strength in a particular situation, large or small. This is the Principle of Reversal applied with a vengeance. The greatest weakness of the Communists and their plans in connection with the American political scene in 1940 was the distrust and detestation by the American people of Roosevelt's foreign policy. Thus the question for the Communists automatically became how to give that the appearance of their greatest strength. So the Communist brain trust went into a huddle, the Communist machine for spreading propaganda went into gear, and millions of people began to state solemnly, as if the thought were original with themselves: "I can't stand Roosevelt, but we *must* support him because of his foreign policy." And the weapon did the job for which it was designed very well indeed.

I LIKE TAFT, BUT . . .

Now let's skip a dozen minor manifestations of the same principle at work, in the same way and for the same purpose, and come to 1952. By that time the Communists were tremendously stronger in America—having been made so by the war and its aftermath exactly as Stalin had foreseen and planned. In fact there is evidence that by 1946 and from then on Stalin had considered himself, through his agents and various forms of

Communist influence and pressures, as in virtual control of our government. But by 1952 a revulsion had set in, and that revulsion had a powerful, courageous, patriotic, and tremendously popular leader, Robert A. Taft. What's more, his incredible vote-getting power, over every dirty trick and pressure play and steamroller of organized opposition which the leftists could muster against him, had just been demonstrated in the senatorial election in Ohio in 1950. If Taft were to be elected president in 1952, there was visibly going to be such a weeding out of Communist agents in our government, and such a reversal of our pro-Communist foreign policy at home and abroad, as to set the Communists back a whole generation in their plans for global conquest. What was worse from their point of view, and was visible to anybody else who would really study the facts realistically as the Communists always do, if Taft were nominated in 1952 he would unquestionably win by one of the greatest landslides in all American history.

The situation was desperate, and it was Taft's vote-getting magic which, above all else, made it desperate. So Taft simply had to be stopped at the nomination stage. (It is in our primary system and our political conventions, which were not set up by the Constitution and are controlled by accumulated political customs, rather than by laws, that the Communists had long before found the Achilles' heel in our whole governmental body.) And again, to stop Taft from being nominated, the Communists behind the scenes pulled out all stops and combined many powerful chords of planning, propaganda, and pressure. But the one that concerns us here, and which became the byword of the whole primary campaign, was a catchphrase made from the same substance, in the same mold, and by the same school of workmen as the slogan we have previously examined. This one went, of course: "I like Taft, but he can't win."

Note the first preliminary step backward, the concession by the Communist designers, in the premise, for the sake of the greater convincingness of the conclusion. It hurt them to have so many millions saying "I like Taft." This was still a bargain price to pay, however, for having the same millions mouth, with the assurance of sad but superior knowledge, "but he can't win."

And the real point for us in this speech, of course, is the way the Principle of Reversal had again been put to work. The greatest danger to the Communists, the greatest weakness in their position, was the overwhelming certainty that Taft, if nominated, would win over any opponent by a huge margin. So they took their greatest weakness and, by daring and bluff—supported in this instance by lies which were staggering as to viciousness, brazenness, and extensiveness—converted that weakness into their greatest item of strength in the particular circumstances.

I LIKE WHAT McCARTHY IS TRYING TO DO, BUT . . .

Let's look at just one more of the products from this mold, before going on to another area. In 1954 the most important thing in the world to the Communists was to destroy McCarthy. Of course the usual line was being spread by the Left that McCarthy was damaging the anti-Communist cause and thus helping the Communists by his supposedly extreme tactics, just as the same nonsense is being peddled about The John Birch Society today. But all you had to do was to read their own literature, where the line was laid down for the faithful, to discover that for about two years they gave the destruction of McCarthy priority and importance over practically everything else on their whole international agenda.

For the thing that bothered them most, the source of their greatest danger and weakness in their battle with McCarthy, was his methods. Of course they didn't like his objective, which was to get rid of Communism. But what frightened them so much was that McCarthy, instead of simply fighting Communism on some ideological or academic level, as almost everybody else had been doing since the pack got rid of Martin Dies and Parnell Thomas, had decided that the way to stop the advance of Communism was to expose individual Communists. And he was right and the Communists knew it better than anybody else.

Of course the Communists and their dupes and allies spread every lie, distortion, and innuendo they could about McCarthy's harshness and browbeating of witnesses and unsupportable charges, and there was little chance to get the truth over to the public through such a well-organized smoke screen of falsehood. What sometimes happened, for instance, was that a witness, under oath, in the preliminary hearing before an executive session of the committee, would give important evidence or tell a story of his own associations and actions which was pertinent to the particular investigation in progress, and would seem cooperative in every way. Then later the same witness, when brought into a public hearing—and visibly because of pressures which had been put on him in the meantime—would turn hostile and completely deny what he had said in executive session. It was the result of such experiences that caused McCarthy to make some pretty sharp—and completely justified—remarks to occasional witnesses, some of them in uniform.

The Communists, of course, used exactly the same kind of lies, defiant disturbances, and planned smears in connection with hearings of the McCarthy subcommittee as they did with regard to the more recent San Francisco hearings of the HCUA, as shown in the film *Operation Abolition.* One of the incidents for which McCarthy was smeared most viciously, just for an illustration, was his accusing Annie Lee Moss of being a Communist. Yet four years later the Pentagon admitted Annie Lee Moss had been a Communist right at the time when McCarthy was being pilloried for saying she was. Basically, and with very minor exceptions indeed, there was nothing wrong with McCarthy's methods from the point of view of the patriotic American. But there was everything wrong with them from the point of view of the Communists. He had found methods which, if allowed to continue, would presently expose enough Communists in high places for the American people to start becoming aware of how rotten things were in areas three thousand miles this side of Denmark. In fact he had already reached the point where he and his methods simply had to be stopped if the whole Communist conspiracy in America were not to be very seriously damaged and perhaps even routed.

So again, in this instance, the Communists designed and set in motion many different methods and forces to accomplish their one end, the destruction of McCarthy. But we are concerned here with only one of those means, the slogan which was devised after exactly the same pattern as the two we have already looked at: "I like what McCarthy is trying to do, but I can't stand his methods." You find in it the same concession for the sake of convincingness, and other revealing similarities to Communist semantic masterpieces. But you also find, which interests us more at the minute, that the Principle of Reversal is the basic strategy of the whole production. The Communists had taken their greatest danger and weakness and, by daring and bluff—again supported in this instance by an unmeasurable campaign of lies and distortions—had converted that weakness into their greatest strength.

There are plenty of other supporting items that might be introduced into this brief, and some of them surprise you by revealing just how long ago the Communists were already effectively at work right here in our country. With small forces but great brilliance they were doing all they could to determine or influence America's course, in war and peace, by catchphrases manufactured to this same formula. But these three examples will have to be enough, and enable us to go on to a look at the Principle of Reversal being employed in still other fields of Communist activity.

V

You find it everywhere. And perhaps a miscellany of scattered instances will be worthwhile before we begin dealing with some fundamental applications, and start approaching both the point and the end of the speech.

IN MISCELLANEOUS APPLICATIONS . . .

Remember, for instance, how, during the Korean War, Chiang Kai-shek had six hundred thousand troops on Formosa, well trained and with their ranks given plenty of backbone by the percentage of veterans who had fought Communists on the mainland. The entry of Red China into the Korean War, theoretically against the United Nations but actually against the United States, supplied just the opportunity for which Chiang and these troops and all of the Chinese patriots on Formosa had been waiting. If these troops started pouring back onto the mainland now—even if at the beginning the invasion had to be in dribbles—and started offering rallying points and leadership for revolts in south and central China while the Reds had their hands so full in Korea, then this operation could easily spread like the proverbial prairie fire. And the mighty revolt, gathering strength and creating renewed hopes, could even start rolling back the Iron Curtain, not only across and from China, but on across the whole Communist-ruled world.

For these and many lesser reasons Chiang Kai-shek's troops simply had to be prevented from even beginning any invasion across the Formosa Strait of the mainland of China. So our Seventh Fleet was kept patrolling these waters for that purpose. But do you remember how the operation was sold to the American people? Our Seventh Fleet was being kept in and near the Formosa Strait to protect Formosa from an invasion by Red Chinese troops from the mainland! Here was the Principle of Reversal applied brazenly and with a vengeance. And being explained so convincingly and with such assurance that probably ninety percent of the people, even in our government, engaged in implementing this clever strategy had no suspicion that they were doing exactly what the Communists wanted.

In Europe after World War II we were stampeded by Communist influences into rapidly reducing our armed forces and leaving all eastern and central Europe wide open for the Communist take-over operations. But the Communists needed time to install their agents and consolidate their power and officially establish themselves in control of so many new satellite nations composed of such hostile people. Even with our tremendously reduced forces, all the United States had to do, *at any point*, was simply and firmly say "Stop," and the Communists could have been held dead in their tracks, or even rolled back from the satellites already subjugated. And there was always some slight chance that the continued absorption of one country after another in Europe by the Soviets, in the period from 1945 to 1950, might wake up enough of the American people to the horror and significance of what was happening. What the Soviets needed so badly was to be let alone for enough time to finish that first step in Lenin's three-part program. So, as one of many precautionary measures taken by the Soviets, the idea was sold to the American people that we were helpless to do anything about the situation until we could get far enough along in rearming or reestablishing our own military strength in Europe and that of our supposedly anti-Communist allies. We were actually told, widely and emphatically, that we had to let the Soviets keep on getting away with this swallowing-of-small-nations process, because we had to make such concessions in order to buy the *time which we needed.*

Like the Burlesque on East River . . .

Or take a look at the current farce being played out by the Kremlin stooges with regard to the United Nations—of which farce Mr. Khrushchev's shoe-banging and other ham acting have been among the most entertaining features. The Communists have now reached the point where they can count on just as complete control of the whole United Nations apparatus as they need. So the most important remaining task in this connection is to pull the United States more completely and definitely into and under the control of the United Nations. And the way to do that, of course, is to convince enough of the American people that the United Nations in general and Dag Hammarskjoeld in particular are actually doing something the Soviets don't want them to do. Which is very easy. They merely apply the Principle of Reversal, and Mr. Khrushchev becomes, for the period necessary to his purpose, the most severe critic of Hammarskjoeld and of the United Nations you could imagine. And he has actually convinced most of those same kinds of people who can also be convinced that the lifelong Communist agent Romulo Betancourt of Venezuela has suddenly become merely a great liberal democrat and an anti-Communist. The Soviets know that there is almost no limit to the innocent gullibility of the American people.

VI

But many such illustrations appear, when presented too hastily, to belong simply in the category of unvarnished lies and deception. The deeper principle so continuously involved is more evident when we come to more basic elements of Communist theory and practice. As for instance in the whole "hungry belly" explanation of Communism.

From the very beginning Communism has been presented as a movement of the proletariat, as a rising of the supposedly shackled and downtrodden poor against the powerful, who were exploiting them. And this itself is one of the biggest lies in all history. For Communism has *always* been imposed from the top down by the very rich, the highly educated, and the politically powerful on the suffering masses whose conditions—even economic conditions—have always been made worse by the tyrannical Communist rule than they were before.

The ordinary happy and innocent American will frequently observe about some multimillionaire or some college president whose activities on behalf of the Communists are obvious: "But of course he couldn't be a Communist himself. He's rich," or

"He's a famous scholar," . . . or whatever the character under discussion may happen to be in the public eye. To which the proper answer is: "Nuts! Where on earth do you think the leaders of Communism come from and always have come from? Almost invariably they have been from the wealthy or best educated classes. A Stalin, who actually arose from the peasantry, is as rare in the ruling Communist circles as is a conscience—and there is no connection between the two."

IN THE BASIC THEME OF COMMUNISM . . .

Conversely, the poorer, less industrialized, less educated, and more correctly described as proletariat any people may be, the more difficult it is to impose on them the chains of Communism, and the more the imposition has to be accomplished and maintained by sheer force and terror—as it has been in China—without the help of infiltrating ideological influences. Czechoslovakia was probably the best educated, most highly industrialized, and was suffering least from hunger and poverty of all the countries in Europe when World War II came. Or certainly it was near the top in these respects. But Czechoslovakia was infinitely easier for the Communists to take over, in just three years after the war, than the Congo would be today if given any similar chance of resistance. And when you look at the Communist strength in America today, you don't find it in the poor, struggling beatniks who by and large comprise the small and insignificant officially presented Communist party. That Communist party exists primarily for propaganda needs in this very pretense. But the strength of the Communist conspiracy lies in the very top social, economic, educational, and political circles of our country. As it always has, everywhere else and in any country. The Principle of Reversal has been used, unmodified in its theory and unchanging in its application, to present Communism as the exact opposite of what it really is, with regard to its basic appeal and purposes, ever since modern Communism was founded as a movement by an intellectual named Karl Marx and a prosperous manufacturer named Engels. And I can find you a lot more Harvard accents in Communist circles in America today than you can find me overalls.

And let's look at some interesting manifestations of this Principle of Reversal in the Communists' whole program of infiltration and of increasing their influence in any country. For where—in what organized segment of our national life—would you least expect to find Communists? Well, considering the fact that it is the avowed goal and compelling necessity of the Communists to wipe out all religion completely, and since the unceasing antagonism of the Communists towards all truly religious bodies is so intense and so well known, it certainly seems that the clergy is the last place in which you would expect to find any appreciable percentage of Communists. And yet two such leading authorities as Herbert Philbrick and Dr. J. B. Matthews, speaking independently and each out of his own separate knowledge and experience, have both been telling us for years that the largest single body of Communists in America is in our Protestant clergy. And I have no slightest doubt that they are right.

Now before the roof starts falling in on me, let me get in three or four most important points concerning that statement and that condition, even though the explanatory comments will be ignored or badly misquoted by the critics. In the first place, there are well over two hundred thousand Protestant ministers in this country, and the estimates I have seen which appeared most trustworthy indicate that about seven thousand of them could fairly be called Comsymps, to use a new word recently coined by a friend of mine. A Comsymp is a man who is either a Communist or a sympathizer with Communist purposes. So the number of Comsymps in the whole Protestant ministry would thus come out as about three percent. And nobody is accusing any of the other ninety-seven percent, or the whole vast body, of anything except—like an awful lot of other good Americans—the gullibility and apathy which allows such a condition to exist.

IN THE CHOICE OF INSTRUMENTALITIES . . .

Next, let's make it clear how even the three percent got where they are. A few years ago I was chosen—for what reason I do not know—to make the commencement speech at an important theological seminary in the East. At that time I offered an explanation of this sinister development with the Protestant clergy, which I repeated more in detail in the course of four lectures which I delivered to an important theological seminary right here in California about a year ago. Since then I have been glad to see that explanation popping up increasingly in various places. For I believe it to be the true explanation, and it is simply this: "Protestant ministers do not become Communists, but Communists do become Protestant ministers."

Of course the very fact that an honest man goes into the ministry means that besides having a deep-rooted faith, he also has strong humanitarian instincts. And it is entirely possible that these noble instincts, leading him at times to think with his heart instead of his head, will cause him to look with favor on socialist theory and practices which are disguised as welfarism. But it is an extremely rare clergyman indeed who would ever be carried by these tendencies to ally himself, knowingly, with an atheistic and criminal conspiracy. The Protestant minister become Communist is of so negligible a quantity that we can simply ignore him in the total picture.

But when some brilliant young man, gradually beguiled by a brilliant professor or two and other Comsymps around, is converted during his college years into a hard-core Communist, the question naturally arises as to how and where he can serve the cause the best. So the young graduate, if he seems adapted to the role of such years of deception, and firm enough to remain a dedicated and disciplined secret agent of the party throughout all of the blasphemous pretenses that will be required of him, may be told to go through a theological seminary, get himself ordained as a minister, and then become—for all ostensible purposes, and in all surface manifestations—the best of all the ministers around. For the others, happy in having found their role of service to God and their fellowmen, will let even normal human ambition to rise in the ranks of the clergy or clerical organizations simply take its proper course. But to the young Communist, his having become a member of the clergy is simply a means to an end. Everything he does is designed to serve the cause of promoting himself, and of thereby ultimately promoting Communist prestige within his church, his community, his whole denomination, and interdenominational church organizations. That, instead of his pretended aims, is his real purpose in life, and some of these Communist wolves in the very midst of the sheep fold carry out that purpose very well indeed. All together they do so with such insidious influence and extensive reach as to produce, within the Protestant clerical hierarchy as a whole, the increasingly disturbing and dangerous developments with which many of you are already familiar.

And of course in this long-range plot we see the Principle of Reversal effectively at work in two different applications. First is with regard to persons. As we have said, the very group where the ordinary American would least suspect, or expect to find, Communists or Communist sympathizers undoubtedly has the largest percentage of Comsymps of any group of similar size in America. But a far more important use of the Principle of Reversal is in the implementation of Communist strategy through this medium. For again they have taken one of their greatest weaknesses and converted it into one of the sources of their greatest strength. The Protestant ministry in America should have been, and by all natural logic would be expected to be, in the very forefront of militant opposition to the Communists; a source of greatest danger to their schemes and a magnifier of their weaknesses. Instead we have seen the top councils of the Protestant ministry become spokesmen and pressure groups for accepting Red China into the family of nations, for promoting the doctrine that capitalism is just as bad as socialism or even outright Communism, and for helping any number of *specific* Communist objectives as well as widely supporting Communist purposes in general.

IN THE CITADEL OF THE ENEMY . . .

And this brings us to the last and most important illustration of the Principle of Reversal at work in the realms of strategy and implementation. The greatest political enemy of Communist imperialism *was* the United States. The greatest obstacle to Communist global conquest *was* the productive, military, and moral power of the United States. The country which the whole world thought, and had every reason to think, was most unshakably opposed to both Communism itself and to the ambitions of the Communists *was* the United States. And so now I hope you have seen, by the Principle of Reversal, and before I even reached the point, how logical it was to the Communists to put such tremendous and continued effort into infiltration of the United States government. Getting their agents into the highest echelons of the government of their most powerful and implacable enemy, and thus converting their greatest weakness and danger into their greatest strength, was clearly indicated as of the very essence of their strategy.

Now I'm not going into the records of Alger Hiss and Harry Dexter White and all their numerous breed that have been exposed. Nor am I going into the administrative gag rule of May 17, 1954, and other factors which have made exposure of such Comsymps in government almost impossible for the past several years. It would require another whole speech simply to remind you of things you have forgotten, and to put them all together in one exhibit, just to show the known and proven measures of Communist accomplishment in this endeavor. And there is neither time nor need for such documentation tonight, for we are dealing with Communist infiltration into our government in only a general way as part of a broader theme and pattern.

THE PRINCIPLE OF REVERSAL . . .

But to make this infiltration sufficiently extensive and sufficiently high was worth to the Communists whatever decades of painstakingly thorough deception and brilliantly insidious effort might be required. As I said earlier in this speech, the Communists themselves seem to have felt that they had reached a satisfactory level of success in this huge and audacious undertaking by at least 1946, if not before. And I should like to agree with them, if you will not jump to any hasty specific conclusions before I explain in a few paragraphs further along. It has become dangerous for me even to imply that Franklin Roosevelt was a *New-Dealer*. But if you will hang on until I make my meaning clear, I'd like to give my own best guess that the Communists have been heavily influencing all major decisions in our government since 1941. The question at all times has been how far they dared to go in the use of their invisible power without stirring up opposition within our government itself which would weaken their influence, and without alerting the American people to increasing awareness of what was really happening. And as protection against these mistakes and dangers the Communists have simply and faithfully lived up to their own self-imposed policy of patient gradualism. For a patient gradualism has been the most important part of the whole practical technique whereby they have been carrying out the Communist global conquest.

But in this case also, as I indicated above, some comments concerning this last illustration are vitally necessary before the roof falls in on me, if it has not already fallen. In the first place, and as much as it may surprise you, I think that at least ninety-eight percent of all the employees of our federal government are loyal and patriotic Americans even today, when I believe the Communist infiltration has reached its highest point. And I think that during the whole period since 1941 there have been more than ninety percent of the total employees of our federal government who never even suspected what was going on, even in the betrayals which they themselves were helping to implement.

The Communists have proved over and over that they are able to control any nation, any population, any organization, or any group with only *about three percent* of its membership. They do this by the skill and determination with which they put their men into the key positions where force and pressure can be exercised. So let's remember that standard ratio and accomplishment. For your speaker has been beaten over the head with the hackneyed charge that he calls everybody who disagrees with him a Communist. And since, according to *Time* magazine and the newspapers, practically everybody disagrees with me these days, that seems like too large an order. May I bring it down to size.

Is Unceasingly at Work . . .

I don't think the Communists yet have anywhere near three percent of federal employees as Comsymps. In other words, while we are sure we disagree vigorously with most of those on the government payroll today on many matters, and especially as to the very functions of government, there is not one in fifty whom we would guess to be a Communist or a Communist sympathizer. But even in Russia itself, the man who called everybody he saw a Communist would be wrong ninety-five percent of the time. The vital question in connection with any group or any government is not how many Communists there are, but where they are. And only a comparatively few thousand Communists concentrated in key departments and agencies of our government could do—and I believe have done—a terrific job of determining both the policies and the actions of those agencies and departments—and hence indirectly of our whole government. If you don't believe it, just look at what has been happening for lo these many years. For a careful study of the history of the fall of Poland, of Yugoslavia, of China, of Cuba, and of a dozen other countries into Communist hands will make one point demonstrably and tragically clear. It is that ever since 1945 or 1946, at best, and perhaps from an earlier date, *our* government has been the most powerful single force supporting the steady worldwide Communist advance—while always pretending, of course, to oppose that advance. The Principle of Reversal never had a more important application, or one that was more profitable to the Communists.

VII

So where does this all take us? Well, back to our original worries about the menace of the Communist conspiracy, of course. But I have hoped that the illustrations and exposition would also serve the additional purpose of building up a clearer understanding of the Principle of Reversal. For now we come to its substance, rather than merely the uses which have been made of it. We must look at what I have called "reversal" as not simply a method of deception, or as a means to an end, but as the end itself.

FOR THE REVERSAL OF ALL HUMAN VALUES . . .

For the effect of Communist total indoctrination seems to be not to condone crime and immorality as ways of accomplishing the ultimate good, but to make crime and immorality appear desirable and praiseworthy in themselves as a part of the ultimate scheme of things. For the recognition of lies and theft and murder, whenever they can be used to advantage in furthering any ambition, or whenever they merely give pleasure to the perpetrator, as perfectly proper for the man who is in position to use them, tends to offset and wipe out any residual respect in the human conscience for such opposites as truth and charity and forgiveness. The net present result, therefore, of social and philosophical acceptance of immorality is to support amorality in theory and complete pragmatism in practice. That kind of spiritual and moral nihilism is apparently an acceptable goal for run-of-the-mill Communist theoreticians. And the widespread and lasting prevalence of any such philosophy would be disastrous enough. But somewhere behind these moral neutralists there seems to be some demonic group or power, self-perpetuating throughout generations, which goes even further. It actually seeks to make hatred, instead of love, the great motivating force, and the ideal to be sustained to the limit of one's dedication, in all the affairs of man.

In this connection—and only in this connection and for this purpose, perhaps—it is worth remembering that Karl Marx was apparently motivated almost entirely by hatred. Being personally one of the most foul individuals who ever lived by practically any standard of appraisal, his whole life was a continuous exercise in hatred of all human beings who were not as foul as himself —and that covered the waterfront. And he built this lifetime of hatred into the foundation of a movement which has caused more crime, more suffering, more destruction of both material and spiritual wealth, and more hopelessness in life, than all other evil movements, in man's total history, combined.

IS THE ESSENCE OF COMMUNIST PURPOSE . . .

What is worse, there obviously have been spiritual successors of Marx who were able to maintain and expand the cult of hatred which he thus established, or which he at least made a sometimes visible phenomenon. Around this seed they have been able to grow ever greater quantities of the bitter fruit which unceasing hatred must produce. We see, everywhere in our world today, the lies and treason, the murders and tortures, the brutal oppression and the merciless exploitation which are the tributes to a god of hatred. We see them replacing the truth and loyalty, the respect for individual life and the compassion for others' pain, the personal responsibility and adherence to the Golden Rule, the belief in man's God-given "upward reach" and in his ever more glorious future on earth, which are the tributes of a morally-climbing man to a God of Love. This is the ultimate Principle of Reversal that is now at work with such frightening and increasing success, through so many thousands of infinitely varied manifestations and implementations of its fundamental purpose.

James Russell Lowell said, in his so-often quoted lines: "Once to every man and nation comes the moment to decide, In the strife of Truth with Falsehood, for the good or evil side." Actually that decision must be faced frequently, not just once, by every man and nation. But there is great variance in the relative importance or the permanent impact of such decisions. It seems beyond dispute, however, that no people, no race, no nation, no generation, ever before had so crucially important a decision to make as faces us today. And our deepest worry of all worries tonight should be, not that we might consciously make the wrong decision, but that we might lose the decision simply by default, through ignorance and gullibility and apathy and fear.

The Communists, and not we, have forced upon this world today a situation where truly "he who is not with me is against me." For the sins of omission by ourselves help the enemy as well as do sins of commission. And the responsibility to those who come after us, which we now face, is staggering in its immensity and its import. But it is my belief that despite all of our fatuous indifference and immoral opportunism of the past, we shall still accept that responsibility in time. What's more, we shall live up to it with all the valor and work and sacrifice and consecration of spirit which are required to save, not only our country and our civilization, but the whole outlook of man for centuries, and possibly for millennia, to come.

In this fight against vastly entrenched evil, some on our side grow weary, and some grow old, and some like myself grow both. But I personally believe we are at the point so beautifully described in St. Paul's Epistle to the Romans: "The night is far spent, the day is at hand: let us therefore cast off the works of darkness, and let us put on the armour of light." We must move forward without doubt and without fear to seize the opportunity that is ours.

Our decision will determine not only the kind of world our descendants are going to live in. It may determine which they will have for an ideal and a taskmaster, hatred or love. The ultimate question we must face in our solemn meditations, and decide by our actions, may hold the outlook and the fate of mankind through uncounted generations. We must decide—or it will surely be decided without us and against us—which we wish our children and their children to worship, the god of hate, or the God of Love, through all the days to be.

Republics and Democracies

As first delivered at the Constitution Day luncheon of We, The People *in Chicago on September 17, 1961. The subheads have been added for the printed version.*

IT IS NOT LIKELY that I shall say anything new here today. If I do, it will be of only minor significance. In all of my remarks, to paraphrase an old quip, the important will not be new, and the new will not be important. For statesmen, historians, and philosophers have been thinking, speaking, and writing on the general subject of which my topic is a part for nearly three thousand years to our definite knowledge, and perhaps for a much longer period of time. Unfortunately there is so much about man's past of which we cannot be sure, for the simple reason that historians themselves occurred rather late in history.

But I can assure you that my attitude towards those who have studied this vast field, and put down their conclusions in many forms, is not that of Donatus, who quipped: *Pereant qui ante nos nostra dixerunt* ("May they perish who have said our things before us"). Whatever pride I might have in exclusive authorship is greatly overweighed by gratitude for all of the observations and thinking and recorded opinions which have been produced by others, of which I am the fortunate heir. And nowhere, outside of his religious meditations, has man bestowed more of his serious thought, throughout his whole history, than on the subject of government. What is more, even within that general subject a preponderant part of man's attention seems to have

89

been fixed on the specific topic as to the proper form and limitation of government when the people try to rule themselves, which concerns us here today.

THEIR HISTORY . . .

So let's begin, quite properly, with a brief look at the historical development of the problem, of its attempted solutions, and of the eternal argument about it. For here, in my opinion, as in every other field of human thought and activity, it is not possible fully to understand the present except as a projection of the past.

II

The first scene in this drama on which the curtain clearly lifts is Greece of the sixth century B.C. The city of Athens was having so much strife and turmoil, primarily as between its various classes, that the wisest citizens felt something of a more permanent nature, rather than just a temporary remedy, had to be developed—to make possible that stability, internal peace, and prosperity which they had already come to expect of life in a civilized society. And through one of those fortunate accidents of history, which surprise us on one side by their rarity and on the other side by ever having happened at all, these citizens of Athens chose an already distinguished fellow citizen named Solon to resolve the problem for both their present and their future. They saw that Solon was given full power over every aspect of government and of economic life in Athens. And Solon, applying himself to the specific job, time, and circumstances, and perhaps without any surmise that he might be laboring for lands and centuries other than his own, proceeded to establish in "the laws of Solon" what amounted to, so far as we know, the first written regulations whereby men ever proposed to govern themselves. Undoubtedly even Solon's decisions and his laws were but projections and syntheses of theories and practices which had already been in existence for a long time. And yet his election as archon of Athens in 594 B.C. can justly be considered as the date of a whole new and huge approach to man's eternal problem of government.

BEGAN IN GREECE . . .

There is no question but that the laws and principles which Solon laid down both foreshadowed and prepared the way for all republics of later ages, including our own. He introduced, into the visible record of man's efforts and progress, the very principle of "government by written and permanent law" instead of "government by incalculable and changeable decrees." (Will Durant) And he himself set forth one of the soundest axioms of all times, that it was a well-governed state "when the people obey the rulers and the rulers obey the laws." This concept, that there were laws which even kings and dictators must observe, was not only new; I think it can be correctly described as "western."

Here was a sharp and important cleavage at the very beginning of our western civilization from the basic concept that always had prevailed in Asia, which concept still prevailed in Solon's day, and which in fact remained unquestioned in the Asiatic mind and empires until long after the fall of the Roman Empire of the East, when Solon had been dead two thousand years.

WHICH STOPPED WITH DEMOCRACY . . .

Unfortunately, while Solon's laws remained in effect in Athens in varying degrees of theory and practice for five centuries, neither Athens nor any of the Greek city-states ever achieved the form of a republic, primarily for two reasons. First, Solon introduced the permanent legal basis for a republican government, but not the framework for its establishment and continuation. The execution, observance, and perpetuation of Solon's laws fell naturally and almost automatically into the hands of tyrants, who ruled Athens for long but uncertain periods of time, through changing forms and administrative procedures for their respective governments. And second, the Greek temperament was too volatile, the whole principle of self-government was too exciting—even through a dictator who might have to be overthrown by force—for the Athenians ever to finish the job Solon had begun, and bind themselves as well as their rulers down to the chains of an unchanging constitution. Even the authority of Solon's laws had to be enforced and thus established by successive tyrants like Pisistratus and Cleisthenes, or they might never have amounted to anything more than a passing dream. The ideal was there, of rule according to written laws; and the fact that those laws were at times and to some extent honored or observed constituted one huge step towards—and fulfilled one prerequisite of—a true republic.

But the second great step of a government framework as fixed and permanent as the basic laws were supposed to be remained for the Romans and other heirs of Greece to achieve. As a consequence Athens—and the other Greek city-states which emulated it—remained politically as democracies, and eventually learned from their own experiences that it was probably the worst of all forms of government.

III

But out of the democracies of Greece, as tempered somewhat by the laws of Solon, there came as a direct spiritual descendant the first true republic the world knew. This was Rome in its earlier centuries after the monarchy had been replaced. The period is usually given as from 509 B.C. to 49 B.C., Rome having got rid of its kings by the first of those dates, and having turned to the caesars by the second. But the really important early date is 454 B.C., when the Roman Senate sent a commission to Greece to study and report on the legislation of Solon. The commission, consisting of three men, did its work well. On its return the

Roman Assembly chose ten men—and hence called the De-cemviri—to rule with supreme power while formulating a new code of laws for Rome. And in 454 B.C. they proposed, and the Assembly adopted, what were called the *Twelve Tables*. This code, based on Solon's laws, became the written constitution of the Roman republic.

BUT ROME INHERITED THIS START . . .

The *Twelve Tables*, "amended and supplemented again and again—by legislation, praetorial edicts, *senatus consulta*, and imperial decrees—remained for nine hundred years the basic law of Rome." (Durant) At least they were in theory, and always to some extent in practice, even after Julius Caesar had founded the empire which was recognized as an empire from the time of Augustus. What was equally important, even before the adoption of the *Twelve Tables*, Rome had already established the framework, with firm periodicity for its public servants, of a republic in which those laws could be, and for a while would be, impartially and faithfully administered.

For, as a Roman named Gaius (and otherwise unknown) was to write in about 160 A.D., "All law pertains to persons, to property, and to procedure." And for a satisfactory government you need as much concern about the implementation of those laws, the governmental agencies through which they are to be administered, and the whole political framework within which those laws form the basis of order and of justice, as with the laws themselves which constitute the original statute books. And the Romans contrived and—subject to the exceptions and changes inflicted on the pattern by the ambitions and cantankerous restlessness of human nature—maintained such a framework in actual practice for nearly five hundred years.

The Romans themselves referred to their government as having a "mixed constitution." By this they meant that it had some of the elements of a democracy, some of the elements of an oligarchy, and some of those of an autocracy; but they also meant that the interests of all the various classes of Roman society were taken into consideration by the Roman constitutional government, rather than just the interests of some one class. Already the Romans were familiar with governments which had been founded by, and were responsible to, one class alone: especially democracies, as of Athens, which at times considered the rights of the proletariat as supreme; and oligarchies, as of Sparta, which were equally biased in favor of the aristocrats. Here again the Roman instinct and experience had led them to one of the fundamental requisites of a true republic.

AND CREATED A REPUBLIC . . .

In summary, the Romans were opposed to tyranny in any form; and the feature of government to which they gave the most thought was an elaborate system of checks and balances. In the early centuries of their republic, whenever they added to the total offices and officeholders, as often as not they were merely increasing the diffusion of power and trying to forestall the potential tyranny of one set of governmental agents by the guardianship or watchdog powers of another group. When the tribunes were set up, for instance, around 350 B.C., their express purpose and duty was to protect the people of Rome against their own government. This was very much as our Bill of Rights was designed by our founding fathers for exactly the same purpose. And other changes in the Roman government had similar aims. The result was a civilization and a government which, by the time Carthage was destroyed, had become the wonder of the world, and which remained so in memory until the nineteenth century—when its glories began receding in the minds of men, because they were surpassed by those of the rising American republic.

Now it should bring more than smiles, in fact it should bring some very serious reflections, to Americans to realize what the most informed and penetrating Romans, of all eras, thought of their early republic.

It is both interesting, and significantly revealing, to find exactly the same arguments going on during the first centuries B.C. and A.D. about the sources of Roman greatness that swirl around us today with regard to the United States. Cicero spoke of their "mixed constitution" as "the best form of government." Polybius, in the second century B.C., had spoken of it in exactly the same terms; and, going further, had ascribed Rome's greatness and triumphs to its form of government. Livy, however, during the days of Augustus, wrote of the virtues that had made Rome great before the Romans had reached the evils of his time, when, as he put it, "We can bear neither our diseases nor their remedies." And those virtues were, he said, "the unity and holiness of family life, the *pietas* [or reverential attitude] of children, the sacred relation of men with the gods at every step, the sanctity of the solemnly pledged word, the stoic self-control and *gravitas* [or serious sense of responsibility]." Doesn't that sound familiar?

But while many Romans gave full credit to both the Roman character and their early environment exactly as we do with regard to American greatness today, the nature and excellence of their early government, and its contribution to the building of Roman greatness, were widely discussed and thoroughly recognized. And the ablest among them knew exactly what they were talking about. "Democracy," wrote Seneca, "is more cruel than wars or tyrants." "Without checks and balances," Dr. Will Durant summarizes one statement of Cicero, "monarchy becomes despotism, aristocracy becomes oligarchy, democracy becomes mob rule, chaos, and dictatorship." And he quotes Cicero verbatim about the man usually chosen as leader by an ungoverned populace, as "someone bold and unscrupulous . . . who curries favor with the people *by giving them other men's property*." (Italics added.)

If that is not an exact description of the leaders of the New Deal, the Fair Deal, and the New Frontier, I don't know where you will find one. What Cicero was bemoaning was the same breakdown of the republic, and of its protection against such

demagoguery and increasing "democracy" as we have been ex-
periencing. This breakdown was under exactly the same kind
of pressures that have been converting the American republic
into a democracy, the only difference being that in Rome those
pressures were not so conspiratorially well organized as they
are in America today. Virgil and many great Romans like him
were, as Will Durant says, well aware that "class war, not
Caesar, killed the Roman Republic." In about 50 B.C., for instance, Sallust had been charging the Roman Senate with placing
property rights above *human rights*. And we are certain that if
Franklin D. Roosevelt had ever heard of Sallust or read one of
Sallust's speeches, he would have told somebody to go out and
hire this man Sallust for one of his ghost writers at once.

IV

About thirty years ago a man named Harry Atwood, who
was one of the first to see clearly what was being done by the
demagogues to our form of government, and the tragic significance of the change, wrote a book entitled *Back to the Republic*.
It was an excellent book except for one shortcoming. Mr. Atwood insisted emphatically, over and over, that ours was the
first republic in history; that American greatness was due to
our founding fathers having given us something entirely new
in history, *the first republic*—which Mr. Atwood described as
the "standard government," or "the golden mean," towards
which all other governments to the right or the left should
gravitate in the future.

Now the truth is that by merely substituting the name Rome
for the name United States, and making similar changes in
nomenclature, Mr. Atwood's book could have been written by
Virgil or by Seneca, with regard to the conversion of the
Roman republic into a democracy. It is only to the extent we
are willing to learn from history that we are able to avoid
repeating its horrible mistakes. And while Mr. Atwood did not
sufficiently realize this fact, fortunately our founding fathers

did. For they were men who knew history well and were determined to profit by that knowledge.

The Greek and Roman Experiences . . .

Also, by the time of the American Revolution and Constitution, the meanings of the words "republic" and "democracy" had been well established and were readily understood. And most of this accepted meaning derived from the Roman and Greek experiences. The two words are not, as most of today's liberals would have you believe—and as most of them probably believe themselves—*parallels* in etymology, or history, or meaning. The word "democracy" (in a political rather than a social sense, of course) had always referred to a type of government, as distinguished from monarchy, or autocracy, or oligarchy, or principate. The word "republic," before 1789, had designated the quality and nature of a government, rather than its structure. When Tacitus complained that "it is easier for a republican form of government to be applauded than realized," he was living in an empire under the caesars and knew it. But he was bemoaning the loss of that adherence to the laws and to the protections of the constitution which made the nation no longer a republic; and not to the fact that it was headed by an emperor.

The word "democracy" comes from the Greek and means literally "government by the people." The word "republic" comes from the Latin *res publica* and means literally "the public affairs." The word "commonwealth," as once widely used, and as still used in the official title of my state, "the Commonwealth of Massachusetts," is almost an exact translation and continuation of the original meaning of *res publica*. And it was only in this sense that the Greeks, such as Plato, used the term that has been translated as "republic." Plato was writing about an imaginary "commonwealth"; and while he certainly had strong ideas about the kind of government this Utopia should have, those ideas were not conveyed nor foreshadowed by his title.

The historical development of the meaning of the word republic might be summarized as follows. The Greeks learned that, as Dr. Durant puts it, "man became free when he recognized that he was subject to law." The Romans applied the formerly general term republic specifically to that system of government in which both the people *and their rulers* were subject to law. That meaning was recognized throughout all later history, as when the term was applied, however inappropriately in fact and optimistically in self-deception to the "Republic of Venice" or to the "Dutch Republic." The meaning was thoroughly understood by our founding fathers. As early as 1775 John Adams had pointed out that Aristotle (representing Greek thought), Livy (whom he chose to represent Roman thought), and Harington (a British statesman) all "define a republic to be . . . a government of laws and not of men." And it was with this full understanding that our constitution-makers proceeded to establish a government which, by its very structure, would require that both the people and their rulers obey certain basic laws—laws which could not be changed without laborious and deliberate changes in the very structure of that government. When our founding fathers established a republic, in the hope, as Benjamin Franklin said, that we could keep it, and when they guaranteed to every state within that republic a republican form of government, they well knew the significance of the terms they were using. And were doing all in their power to make the features of government signified by those terms as permanent as possible. They also knew very well indeed the meaning of the word democracy, and the history of democracies; and they were deliberately doing everything in their power to avoid for their own times, and to prevent for the future, the evils of a democracy.

Let's look at some of the things they said to support and clarify this purpose. On May 31, 1787, Edmund Randolph told his fellow members of the newly assembled Constitutional Convention that the object for which the delegates had met was "to provide a cure for the evils under which the United States labored; that in tracing these evils to their origin every man had found it in the turbulence and trials of democracy. . . ."

Were Well Known to Our Founding Fathers . . .

The delegates to the convention were clearly in accord with this statement. At about the same time another delegate, Elbridge Gerry, said: "The evils we experience flow from the excess of democracy. The people do not want [that is, do not lack] virtue; but are the dupes of pretended patriots." And on June 21, 1788, Alexander Hamilton made a speech in which he stated:

It had been observed that a pure democracy if it were practicable would be the most perfect government. Experience had proved that no position is more false than this. The ancient democracies in which the people themselves deliberated never possessed one good feature of government. Their very character was tyranny; their figure deformity.

At another time Hamilton said: "We are a Republican Government. Real liberty is never found in despotism or in the extremes of Democracy." And Samuel Adams warned: "Remember, Democracy never lasts long. It soon wastes, exhausts and murders itself! There never was a democracy that 'did not commit suicide.' "

James Madison, one of the members of the convention who was charged with drawing up our Constitution, wrote as follows:

. . . democracies have ever been spectacles of turbulence and contention; have ever been found incompatible with personal security, or the rights of property; and have in general been as short in their lives as they have been violent in their deaths.

Who Established Our Republic . . .

Madison and Hamilton and Jay and their compatriots of the convention prepared and adopted a constitution in which they nowhere even mentioned the word democracy, not because they were not familiar with such a form of government, but because they were. The word democracy had not occurred in the Declaration of Independence, and does not appear in the constitution of a single one of our fifty states—which constitutions are derived mainly from the thinking of the founding fathers of the republic—for the same reason. They knew all about democracies, and if they had wanted one for themselves and their posterity, they would have founded one. Look at all the elaborate system of checks and balances which they established; at the carefully worked-out protective clauses of the Constitution itself, and especially of the first ten amendments, known as the Bill of Rights; at the effort, as Jefferson put it, to "bind men down from mischief by the chains of the Constitution," and thus to solidify the rule not of men but of laws. All of these steps were taken deliberately to avoid and to prevent a democracy, or any of the worst features of a democracy, in the United States of America.

V

And so our republic was started on its way. And for well over a hundred years our politicians, statesmen, and people remembered that this was a republic, not a democracy, and knew what they meant when they made that distinction. Again, let's look briefly at some of the evidence.

Washington, in his first inaugural address, dedicated himself to "the preservation . . . of the republican model of government." Thomas Jefferson, our third president, was the founder of the Democratic party; but in his first inaugural address, although he referred several times to the republic or the republican form of government, he did not use the word democracy a single time. And John Marshall, who was chief justice of the Supreme Court from 1801 to 1835, said: "Between a balanced republic and a democracy, the difference is like that between order and chaos."

Throughout all of the nineteenth century and the very early part of the twentieth, while America as a republic was growing great and becoming the envy of the whole world, there were plenty of wise men, both in our country and outside of it, who pointed to the advantages of a republic, which we were enjoying, and warned against the horrors of a democracy, into which we might fall. Around the middle of that century, Herbert Spencer, the great English philosopher, wrote, in an article on "The Americans": "The Republican form of government is the highest form of government; but because of this it requires the highest type of human nature—a type nowhere at present existing." And in truth we have not been a high enough type to preserve the republic we then had, which is exactly what he was prophesying.

AND THE DANGERS OF A DEMOCRACY . . .

Thomas Babington Macaulay said: "I have long been convinced that institutions purely democratic must, sooner or later, destroy liberty or civilization, or both." And we certainly seem to be in a fair way today to fulfill his dire prophecy. Nor was Macaulay's contention a mere personal opinion without intellectual roots and substance in the thought of his times. Nearly two centuries before, Dryden had already lamented that "no government had ever been, or ever can be, wherein time-servers and blockheads will not be uppermost." And as a result, he had spoken of nations being "drawn to the dregs of a democracy." While in 1795 Immanuel Kant had written: "Democracy is necessarily despotism."

In 1850 Benjamin Disraeli, worried as was Herbert Spencer at what was already being foreshadowed in England, made a speech to the British House of Commons in which he said:

If you establish a democracy, you must in due time reap the fruits of a democracy. You will in due season have great impatience of public burdens, combined in due season with great increase of public expenditure. You will in due season have wars entered into from passion and not from reason; and you will in due season submit to peace ignominiously sought and ignominiously obtained, which will diminish your authority and perhaps endanger your independence. You will in due season find your property is less valuable, and your freedom less complete.

Disraeli could have made that speech with even more appropriateness before a joint session of the American Congress in 1935. And in 1870 he had already come up with an epigram which is strikingly true for the United States today. "The world is weary," he said, "of statesmen whom democracy has degraded into politicians."

But even in Disraeli's day there were similarly prophetic voices on this side of the Atlantic. In our own country James Russell Lowell showed that he recognized the danger of unlimited majority rule by writing:

> Democracy gives every man
> The right to be his own oppressor.

W. H. Seward pointed out that "Democracies are prone to war, and war consumes them." This is an observation certainly borne out during the past fifty years exactly to the extent that we have been becoming a democracy and fighting wars, with each trend as both a cause and an effect of the other one. And Ralph Waldo Emerson issued a most prophetic warning when he said: "Democracy becomes a government of bullies tempered by editors." If Emerson could have looked ahead to the time when so many of the editors would themselves be a part of, or sympathetic to, the gang of bullies as they are today, he would have been even more disturbed. And in the 1880's Governor Seymour of New York said that the merit of our Constitution was not that it promotes democracy, but checks it.

Across the Atlantic again, a little later, Oscar Wilde once contributed this epigram to the discussion: "Democracy means simply the bludgeoning of the people, by the people, for the people." While on this side, and after the first World War had made the degenerative trend in our government so visible to any penetrating observer, H. L. Mencken wrote: "The most popular man under a democracy is not the most democratic man, but the most despotic man. The common folk delight in the exactions of such a man. They like him to boss them. Their natural gait is the goosestep." While Ludwig Lewisohn observed: "Democracy, which began by liberating man politically, has developed a dangerous tendency to enslave him through the tyranny of majorities and the deadly power of their opinion."

Were Well Understood . . .

But it was a great Englishman, G. K. Chesterton, who put his finger on the basic reasoning behind all the continued and determined efforts of the Communists to convert our republic into a democracy. "You can never have a revolution," he said, "in order to establish a democracy. You must have a democracy in order to have a revolution."

And in 1931 the duke of Northumberland, in his booklet *The History of World Revolution*, stated:

The adoption of Democracy as a form of Government by all European nations is fatal to good Government, to liberty, to law and order, to respect for authority, and to religion, and must eventually produce a state of chaos from which a new world tyranny will arise.

While an even more recent analyst, Archibald E. Stevenson, summarized the situation as follows:

De Tocqueville once warned us that: "If ever the free institutions of America are destroyed, that event will arise from the unlimited tyranny of the majority." But a majority will never be permitted to exercise such "unlimited tyranny" so long as we cling to the American ideals of republican liberty and turn a deaf ear to the siren voices now calling us to democracy. This is not a question relating to the *form* of government. That can always be changed by constitutional amendment. It is one affecting the underlying philosophy of our system—a philosophy which brought new dignity to the individual, more safety for minorities and greater justice in the administration of government. We are in grave danger of dissipating this splendid heritage through mistaking it for democracy.

And there have been plenty of other voices to warn us.

VI

So—how did it happen that we have been allowing this gradual destruction of our inheritance to take place? And when did it start? The two questions are closely related.

For not only every democracy, but certainly every republic, bears within itself the seeds of its own destruction. The difference is that for a soundly conceived and solidly endowed republic it takes a great deal longer for those seeds to germinate and the plants to grow. The American republic was bound—is still bound—to follow in the centuries to come the same course to destruction as did Rome. But our real ground of complaint is that we have been pushed down the demagogic road to disaster by conspiratorial hands far sooner and far faster than would have been the results of natural political evolution.

UNTIL THE FABIAN CONSPIRATORS . . .

These conspiratorial hands first got seriously to work in this country in the earliest years of the twentieth century. The Fabian philosophy and strategy was imported to America from England, as it had been earlier to England from Germany. Some of the members of the Intercollegiate Socialist Society, founded in 1905, and some of the members of the League for Industrial Democracy into which it grew, were already a part of, or affiliated with, an international Communist conspiracy planning to make the United States a portion of a one-world Communist state. Others saw it as possible and desirable merely to make the United States a separate socialist Utopia. But they all knew and agreed that to do either they would have to destroy both the constitutional safeguards and the underlying philosophy which made it a republic. So, from the very beginning the whole drive to convert our republic into a democracy was in two parts. One part was to make our people come to believe that we had, and were supposed to have, a democracy. The second part was actually and insidiously to be changing the republic into a democracy.

The first appreciable and effective progress in both directions began with the election of Woodrow Wilson. Of Wilson it could accurately have been said, as Tacitus had said of some Roman counterpart: "By common consent, he would have been deemed capable of governing had he never governed." Since he did become the president of the United States for two terms, however, it is hard to tell how much of the tragic disaster of those years was due to the conscious support by Wilson himself of Communist purposes, and how much to his being merely a dupe and a tool of Colonel Edward Mandell House. But at any rate it is under Wilson that, for the first time, we see the power of the American presidency being used to support Communist schemers and Communist schemes in other countries—as especially, for instance, in Mexico, and throughout Latin America.

It was under Wilson, of course, that the first huge parts of the Marxian program, such as the progressive income tax, were incorporated into the American system. It was under Wilson that the first huge legislative steps to break down what the Romans would have called our "mixed constitution" of a republic, and convert it into the homogenous jelly of a democracy, got under way with such measures as the direct election of senators. And it was under Wilson that the first great propaganda slogan was coined and emblazoned everywhere to make Americans start thinking favorably of democracies and forget that we had a republic. This was, of course, the slogan of the first World War: "To make the world safe for democracy." If enough Americans had, by those years, remembered enough of their own history, they would have been worrying about how to make the world safe *from* democracy. But the great deception and the great conspiracy were already well under way.

UNDER WILSON AND THEN ROOSEVELT . . .

The conspirators had to proceed slowly and patiently, nevertheless, and to have their allies and dupes do the same. For in the first place the American people could not have been swept too fast and too far in this movement without enough alarms being sounded to be heard and heeded. And in the second place, after the excitement of World War I had sunk into the past, and America was returning to what Harding called "normalcy," there was a strong revulsion against the whole binge of demagoguery and crackpot idealism which had been created under Woodrow Wilson, and which had been used to give us this initial push on the road towards ultimate disaster. And during this period from 1920 until the so-called great depression could be deliberately accentuated, extended, and increased to suit the purposes of the Fabian conspirators, there was simply a germination period for the seeds of destruction which the conspirators had planted. Not until Franklin D. Roosevelt came to power in 1933 did the whole Communist-propelled and Communist-managed drive again begin to take visible and tangible and positive steps in their program to make the United States ultimately succumb to a one-world Communist tyranny. Most conservative Americans are today well aware of many of those steps and of their significance; but there are still not enough who realize how important to Communist plans was the two-pronged drive to convert the American republic into a democracy and to make the American people accept the change without even knowing there had been one. From 1933 on, however, that drive and that change moved into high gear, and have been kept there ever since.

Let's look briefly at just two important and specific pieces of tangible evidence of this drive, and of its success in even those early years.

In 1928 the U.S. Army Training Manual, used for all of

our men in army uniform, gave them the following quite accurate definition of a democracy:

A government of the masses. Authority derived through mass meeting or any form of "direct" expression. Results in mobocracy. Attitude toward property is communistic—negating property rights. Attitude toward law is that the will of the majority shall regulate, whether it be based upon deliberation or governed by passion, prejudice, and impulse, without restraint or regard to consequences. Results in demagogism, license, agitation, discontent, anarchy.

That was in 1928. Just when that true explanation was dropped, and through what intermediate changes the definition went, I have not had sufficient time and opportunity to learn. But compare that 1928 statement with what was being said in the same place for the same use by 1952. In *The Soldiers Guide*, Department of the Army Field Manual, issued in June of 1952, we find the following:

Meaning of democracy. *Because the United States is a democracy*, the majority of the people decide how our government will be organized and run—and that includes the Army, Navy, and Air Force. The people do this by electing representatives, and these men and women then carry out the wishes of the people. [Italics added.]

Now obviously this change from basic truth to superficial demagoguery in the one medium for mass indoctrination of our youth which has been available to the federal government until such time as it achieves control over public education, did not just happen by accident. It was part of an overall design, which became both extensive in its reach and rapid in its execution from 1933 on. Let's look at another less important but equally striking illustration.

Former Governor Lehman of New York, in his first inaugural message in 1933, did not once use the word democracy. The poison had not yet reached into the reservoirs from which flowed his political thoughts. In his inaugural message of 1935 he used the word democracy twice. The poison was beginning to work. In his similar message of 1939 he used the word democracy, or a derivative thereof, *twenty-five* times. And less than a year later, on January 3, 1940, in his annual message to the New York legislature he used it thirty-three times. The poison was now permeating every stream of his political philosophy.

GRADUALLY CHANGED OUR THINKING . . .

By today that same poison has been diffused in an effective dosage through almost the whole body of American thought about government. Newspapers write ringing editorials declaring that this is and always was a democracy. In pamphlets and books and speeches, in classrooms and pulpits and over the air, we are besieged with the shouts of the liberals and their political henchmen, all pointing with pride to our being a democracy. Many of them even believe it. Here we have a clear-cut sample of the Big Lie which has been repeated so often and so long that it is increasingly accepted as truth. And never was a Big Lie spread more deliberately for more subversive purposes. What is even worse, because of their unceasing efforts to destroy the safeguards, traditions, and policies which made us a republic, and partly because of this very propaganda of deception, what they have been shouting so long is gradually *becoming* truth. Despite Mr. Warren and his Supreme Court and all of their allies, dupes, and bosses, we are not yet a democracy. But the fingers in the dike are rapidly becoming fewer and less effective. And a great many of the pillars of our republic have already been washed away.

Since 1912 we have seen the imposition of a graduated income tax, as already mentioned. Also, as mentioned, the direct election of senators. We have seen the Federal Reserve System established and then become the means of giving our central government absolute power over credit, interest rates, and the quantity and value of our money; and we have seen the federal government increasingly use this means and this power to take money from the pockets of the thrifty and put it in the hands of the thriftless, to expand bureaucracy, increase its huge debts and deficits, and to promote socialistic purposes of every kind.

We have seen the federal government increase its holdings of land by tens of millions of acres, and go into business as a substitute for and in competition with private industry to the extent that in many fields it is now the largest—and in every case the most inefficient—producer of goods and services in the nation. And we have seen it carry the socialistic control of agriculture to such extremes that the once vaunted independence of our farmers is now a vanished dream. We have seen a central government taking more and more control over public education, over communications, over transportation, over every detail of our daily lives.

AND OUR REPUBLIC ITSELF . . .

We have seen a central government promote the power of labor union bosses, and in turn be supported by that power, until it has become entirely too much a government of and for one class, which is exactly what our founding fathers wanted most to prevent.

We have seen the firm periodicity of the tenure of public office terrifically weakened by the four terms as president of Franklin D. Roosevelt, something which would justly have horrified and terrified the founders of our republic. It was the fact that in Greece the chief executive officer stayed in power for long periods which did much to prevent the Greeks ever achieving a republic. In Rome it was the rise of the same tendency, under Marius and Sulla and Pompey, and as finally carried to its logical state of life rule under Julius Caesar, which at last destroyed the republic even though its forms were left. And that, of course, is precisely one reason why the Communists and so many of their liberal dupes wanted third and fourth terms for FDR. They knew they were thus helping to destroy the American republic.

We have seen both the executive department and the Supreme Court override and break down the clearly established rights of the states and state governments, of municipal governments, and of so many of those diffusers of power so carefully protected by the Constitution. Imagine, for instance, what James Madison would have thought of the federal government telling the city of Newburgh, New York, that it had no control over the abuse by the shiftless of its welfare handouts.

We have seen an utterly unbelievable increase in government by appointive officials and bureaucratic agencies—a development entirely contrary to the very concept of government expounded and materialized by our Constitution. And we have seen the effective checking and balancing of one department of our government by another department almost completely disappear.

UNTIL WE ARE NOW IN DANGER . . .

James Madison, in trying to give us a republic instead of a democracy, wrote that "the accumulation of all powers, legislative, executive, and judicial, in the same hands, whether of one, a few, or many, and whether hereditary, self-appointed, or elective, may justly be denounced as the very definition of tyranny." The whole problem for the liberal establishment that runs our government today, and has been running it for many years regardless of the labels worn by successive administrations, has not been any divergence of beliefs or of purposes between the controlling elements of our executive, legislative, or judicial branches. For twenty years, despite the heroic efforts of men like Taft to stop the trend, these branches have been acting increasingly in complete accord, and obviously according to designs laid down for them by the schemers and plotters behind the scenes. And their only question has been as to how fast the whole tribe dared to go in advancing the grand design. We do not yet have a democracy simply because it takes a lot of time and infinite pressures to sweep the American people all of the way into so disastrous an abandonment of their governmental heritage.

In the Constitution of the American republic there was a deliberate and very extensive and emphatic division of governmental power for the very purpose of preventing unbridled majority rule. In our Constitution governmental power is divided among three separate branches of the national government, three separate branches of state governments, and the peoples of the several states. And the governmental power, which is so divided, is sometimes exclusive, sometimes concurrent, sometimes limited, at all times specific, and sometimes reserved. Ours was truly, and purposely, a "mixed constitution."

OF BECOMING A DEMOCRACY . . .

In a democracy there is a centralization of governmental power in a simple majority. And that, visibly, is the system of government which the enemies of our republic are seeking to impose on us today. Nor are we "drifting" into that system, as Harry Atwood said in 1933, and as many would still have us believe. We are being insidiously, conspiratorially, and *treasonously* led by deception, by bribery, by coercion, and by fear to destroy a republic that was the envy and model for all of the civilized world.

VII

Finally, let's look briefly at two or three important characteristics of our republic, and of our lives under the republic, which were unique in all history up to the present time.

First, our republic has offered the greatest opportunity and encouragement to *social democracy* the world has ever known. Just as the Greeks found that obedience to law made them free, so Americans found that social democracy flourished best in the absence of political democracy. And for sound reasons. For the safeguards to person and property afforded by a republic, the stable framework which it supplied for life and labor at *all* levels, and the resulting constant flux of individuals from one class into another made caste impossible and snobbery a joke.

TO SAVE TRUE SOCIAL DEMOCRACY . . .

In the best days of our republic Americans were fiercely proud of the fact that rich and poor met on such equal terms in so many ways, and without the slightest trace of hostility. The whole thought expressed by Burns in his famous line "a man's a man for a' that" has never been accepted more unquestioningly, nor lived up to more truly, than in America in those wonderful decades before the intellectual snobs and power-drunk bureaucrats of our recent years set out to make everybody theoretically equal (except to themselves) by legislation and coercion. And I can tell you this. When you begin to find that Jew and Gentile, white and colored, rich and poor, scholar and laborer, are genuinely and almost universally friendly to one another again—instead of going through all the silly motions of a phony equality forced upon them by increasing political democracy—you can be sure that we have already made great strides in the restoration of our once glorious republic.

And for a very last thought, let me point out what seems to me to be something about the underlying principles of the American republic which really was new in the whole philosophy of government. In man's earlier history, and especially in the Asiatic civilizations, all authority rested in the king or the conqueror by virtue of sheer military power. The subjects of the king had absolutely no rights except those given them by the king. And such laws or constitutional provisions as did grow up were concessions wrested from the king or given by him out of his own supposedly ultimate authority. In more modern European states, where the complete military subjugation of one nation by another was not so normal, that ultimate authority of the ruler came to rest on the theory of the divine right of kings, or in some instances and to some extent on power specifically bestowed on rulers by a pope as the representative of divinity.

In the meantime the truly western current of thought, which had begun in Greece, was recurrently, intermittently, and haltingly gaining strength. It was that the people of any nation owed their rights to the government which they themselves had established and which owed its power ultimately to their consent. Just what rights any individual citizen had was properly determined by the government which all of the citizens had established, and those rights were subject to a great deal of variations in different times and places under different regimes. In other words, the rights of individuals were still changeable rights, derived from government, even though the power and authority and rights of the government were themselves derived from the total body of the people.

AND OUR "UNALIENABLE RIGHTS" . . .

Then both of these basic theories of government, the eastern and the western, were really amended for all time by certain principles enunciated in the American Declaration of Independence. Those principles became a part of the very foundation of our republic. And they said that man has certain *unalienable rights* which do not derive from government at all. Under this theory not only the sovereign conqueror, but the sovereign people, are restricted in their power and authority by man's natural rights, or by the divine rights of the individual man. And those certain unalienable and divine rights cannot be abrogated by the vote of a majority any more than they can by the decree of a conqueror. The idea that the vote of a people, no matter how nearly unanimous, makes or creates or determines what is right or just becomes as absurd and unacceptable as the idea that right and justice are simply whatever a king says they are. Just as the early Greeks learned to try to have their rulers and themselves abide by the laws they had themselves established, so man has now been painfully learning that there are more permanent and lasting laws which cannot be changed by either sovereign kings or sovereign people, but which must be observed by both. And that government is merely a convenience, superimposed on Divine Commandments and on the natural laws that flow only from the Creator of man and man's universe.

Now that principle seems to me to be the most important addition to the theory of government in all history. And it has, as I said, at least tacitly been recognized as a foundation stone and cardinal tenet of the American republic. But of course any such idea that there are unchangeable limitations on the power of the people themselves is utterly foreign to the theory of a democracy, and even more impossible in the practices of one. And this principle may ultimately be by far the most significant of all the many differences between a republic and a democracy. For in time, under any government, without that principle slavery is inevitable, while with it slavery is impossible. And the American republic has been the first great example of that principle at work.

We Must Keep Our Republic . . .

In summary, I personally think that, as I said in the Blue Book of The John Birch Society, democracy is a weapon of demagoguery and a perennial fraud. I think that a constitutional republic is the best of all forms of government man has yet devised. Our founding fathers thought so too, and the wisest Romans had already come to that same conclusion. So I am in excellent company. It is company which we hope more and more Americans will join. To that end we are saying everywhere we can, and asking all of you and tens of thousands to say with us: This is a Republic, not a Democracy. Let's keep it that way!

More Stately Mansions

As delivered at the Conrad Hilton Hotel in Chicago on June 5, 1964. The subheads have been added for the printed version.

ALMOST EXACTLY TWO THOUSAND YEARS AGO Marcus Tullius Cicero, obviously referring to Julius Caesar, said that an ungoverned populace usually chose as its leader "someone bold and unscrupulous . . . who curries favor with the people by giving them other men's property."

On January 15, 1964, in a speech at the White House, President Lyndon B. Johnson said: "We are going to try to take all of the money that we think is unnecessarily being spent and take it from the 'haves' and give it to the 'have nots' that need it so much." Now Lyndon Johnson is hardly a Julius Caesar, but maybe he ought to get some ghost writers who have read a bit more history.

Or guess who made this statement:

I want all to have a share of everything, and all property to be in common; there will no longer be either rich or poor; no longer shall we see one man harvesting vast tracts of land, while another has not ground enough to be buried in . . . I intend that there shall only be one and the same condition of life for all. . . . I shall begin by making land, money, everything that is private property, common to all.

If you guessed Eleanor Roosevelt you are badly wrong. For these are the words which, about four hundred years before Christ, the playwright Aristophanes put in the mouth of one of

his female characters as a means of satirizing the communists—
and we do mean communists—of his day. And at just about that
same time, 400 B.C., Isocrates remarked that the enemies of
Athens certainly ought to pay the Athenian Assembly for con-
vening so frequently, because of all the mistakes that the assembly made.

We could readily fill a hundred pages with similar repetitions
by history of men's venal hypocrisies. But that is not our assign-
ment tonight. We have merely introduced those samples to show
why we go back quite a distance into the past to creep up on
the present. For this will be a serious speech. Some of it may
not even be too easy to digest, when so much compacted substance is thrown at you so fast. But there have never been more
serious times. And in discussing with you the problems and
dangers which we face, and the proposed answers and remedies
based primarily on man's past experience, I want to go far
enough back to start from a solid base. So please bear with me
while I sound like a history lesson for the first part of this dis-
course.

THE OLDEST AND LONGEST WAR . . .

Confucius said that all men are born good. Leibnitz said
that everything is for the best in this best of all possible worlds.
Some theologians will dispute both statements as heresy. Some
philosophers will proclaim that neither sentence means anything
except as a study in definitions. And some plain everyday
cynics will tell you that both pronouncements are gross ex-
aggerations, to say the least.

We have no wish to get into any of those arguments. We
merely want to point out that, however little some of us know
about the ultimate beginnings and bases of the struggle, there
has been a visible and unceasing battle between the forces of
evil and the forces of good, both among all mankind and even
in the nature of individual man, from as far back as we can see
in history. And while we do not agree with James Russell

Lowell that Right has *always* been on the scaffold and Wrong forever on the throne, we do admit that Wrong has at least *seemed* to be victorious during many long hard stretches of the way.

In fact some blasé wit has reported the current war news in that struggle between good and evil in a limerick which we do not remember exactly, which we quote without intending any irreverence, and which—as incurable optimists—we certainly do not accept or endorse. But it goes approximately as follows:

> God's plan made a hopeful beginning,
> Till man spoiled his chances by sinning.
>   We trust that the story
>   Will end in God's glory,
> But at present the other side's winning.

Now this eternal war between good and evil has been fought on many fronts, in many ways, and with many weapons. We wish to deal tonight with just one front. This is the area in which the forces of evil have fought under the banner of collectivism, and the forces of good have defended themselves as well as they could under the banner of individual rights and responsibilities.

We occasionally catch glimpses of confused and confusing engagements on this front, even in the ancient civilizations of Egypt and of the Tigris-Euphrates valley. But in those days and places the tyranny of government over its subjects was quite frankly imposed and maintained by stark military might. There was no pretense about government owing its power to the consent of the governed. With regard to early Asiatic rulers, anyway, Carlyle was writing doubtful etymology but quite sound sociology in the famous line which is usually paraphrased, "He is king who can." So, in the age of the pharaohs, the battle lines between good and evil, or even between freedom and tyranny, were seldom drawn on the front between individualism and collectivism.

WITH REINFORCEMENTS ON THE RIGHT . . .

By the time of Solon, however, in the first half of the sixth century B.C., a new theory was being accepted, that government owed its power to the consent of those governed. This was the basic theme of democracy, and in many ways it represented a huge advance over the Asiatic principle of governmental power resting on sheer might. But unfortunately, the forces of evil early recognized that the consent of the governed could readily be reduced in practice to the whim of the mob; that it could be made to derive from the bigotry of the ignorant, the enviousness of the irresponsible, the greed of the shiftless, the self-righteousness of the *unco guid*, and even from the manipulation by clever agents of the quite temporary passions of a volatile people. The consent of the governed soon became merely the mechanics by which demagogues put themselves in power.

Since these demagogues, to obtain the support of the mobs and masses, usually made the natural pitch of promising to take from the haves and give to the have-nots, and since increasing agencies of government were always necessary to handle and effectuate these transfers, the meshing of demagoguery and collectivism was as inevitable as sunrise. And so the forces of evil, which appeal to the laziness, the selfishness, the rapacity, and to all of the criminal tendencies of man, early became the continuing matrix of these recurrent alliances between demagogues and the rabble. For the forces of evil sought always to destroy or weaken man's slowly building traditions of morality, of property rights, of the rights and responsibilities of the individual. And there was no surer nor quicker way to damage these *mores* than through the government of tyrants who derived their power from mob instincts, which placed no value on the individual.

The early growth in the Greek world of city-state tyrannies based on this process was due in part to Solon's having been preoccupied with a system of laws, without consideration for a system of government through which those laws were to be enforced. There was not even the attempt, so valued by Thomas Jefferson twenty-four hundred years later, to bind successive rulers down by the chains of a constitution. With the result that from the time of Solon, until oriental ideas of government by raw military power were reimposed by Alexander the Great near the end of the fourth century B.C., democracy ran wild throughout the Greek world. Any ambitious and ruthless enough criminal could make himself the tyrant—as these rulers of city-states were quite properly called—by masquerading his crimes as still further advances of collectivism for the good of the people. With one interesting result that was quite beneficial to any real future progress of mankind in connection with problems of social organization. It was that by the beginning of the Christian era the most intelligent Romans had learned, even more from the history of the Greeks than from the experiences of their own country, that an unbridled democracy was the worst of all forms of government.

In the meantime, the Romans had devised the first real republic in history—with that diffusion of governmental power and system of checks and balances which were designed to protect a people from the results of their own ephemeral follies. So that by the time the Romans adopted the laws of Solon in 454 B.C., they had a permanent framework of government through which these laws were to be maintained, enforced, and made binding on rulers as well as on those ruled. Unfortunately, however, the forces of evil had already learned the irresistible power of the collectivist appeals; and the legal guard rails erected by pioneering forefathers could only hold back the mob for a while. They could not stop it from gradually trampling down these barriers in recurrent and ever greater stampedes towards socialist morasses, which were pictured by the collectivists of course as greener pastures.

In fact, most of the demagogic ideological appeals which are used by the collectivists as their strongest weapons to this very day were already commonplace by the time the Roman republic itself had been converted by successive criminal tyrants into a democracy. The principle of "agrarian reform," which is a fancy liberal name for stealing land from its owners and distributing it to the far more numerous tenants, was used by the Gracchi in the second century B.C. as opportunistically as by Mao Tse-tung twenty-one hundred years later, and by dozens of equal scoundrels in between. And the extension of the vote to new classes in order to dilute the influence of the solider citizenry and increase the weight of the rootless mobs was advocated by the Gracchi with the same arguments used by those who wish to reduce the voting age today to include youthfully irresponsible college pranksters who set "records" by piling forty-five of themselves into one bed.

By the turn of the first century B.C., Gaius Marius could have given Charles de Gaulle lessons in how to murder and imprison his anti-collectivist enemies by quasi-legal means; and by 50 B.C. that tribune of the pee-pul Gaius Sallust could have taught economic demagoguery to Huey Long and simultaneous personal fortune grabbing to Eleanor Roosevelt. By now the forces of evil had learned well, from massive experience, to use government as the instrumentality through which to achieve their ambitions, and to use the demagogic appeal of bread and circuses for the masses as a means of controlling that instrumentality.

THE OLD IS NEW, BUT . . .

The phrase that there is nothing new under the sun was itself once new. Everything about the deceptive, dishonest, and destructive processes of collectivism has, of course, been new at some point in the gradual evolution of the massive sociological machinery with which the criminal manipulators now pursue their own power and happiness. But since the time when a caesar became *augustus*, there has been little except refinements and enlargements in the basic tricks of the demagogic trade.

The difference between the coin clipping by Roman emperors, the printing of paper money without substance under it by practically all modern governments, and the dilution of the value of our own currency by the more intricate shenanigans of our Federal Reserve System is entirely a difference in mechanics, and not in either morality or purpose. These operations are all simply the means by which a government brazenly but insidiously steals from its own people for the benefit of those who control the government.

The price controls and wages controls and all of the similar procedures of economic regimentation for burying the rights and responsibilities of individuals under the huge palimpsest of government's rights and responsibilities, as inaugurated by Diocletian in around 300 A.D., were necessarily changed in scope, but not at all in principle, when reestablished as Franklin Roosevelt's New Deal sixteen hundred years later.

Similarly, while that powerful modern slogan for the philosophical defense of collectivism, namely "the greatest good of the greatest number," appears to have been created in approximately that form by Francis Hutchinson about 1720 and made the basis of so-called philosophic radicalism by Jeremy Bentham and the Millses only a century and a quarter ago, there is little changed in it from the thoughts with which Plato had infected the minds of men more than two thousand years before. Plato, Bentham, and the Millses all undoubtedly had the best of intentions. But that fact does not alter one bit the uses to which their fantastic misconceptions as to the sources of both progress and true humanitarianism in human society have been put by megalomaniacal or cold-blooded criminals who sought only their own greatest gain under the pretense of these ideals.

Of course there were contemporaries of John Stuart Mill who saw the fallacies in the utilitarian philosophy as a guide to government. Bulwer Lytton acidly commented that "The greatest happiness of the greatest number is best secured by a prudent consideration for Number One." And Herbert Spencer, in direct reference to one of the rising methods of the collectivists for shifting power and responsibilities into government

hands—which he called "State Tamperings with Money Banks"
—came up with one of the most penetrating epigrams of all
time. "The ultimate effect," he said, "of shielding men from
the effects of folly is to fill the world with fools." But there is
little basically different, even in these criticisms of the excuses
and the mechanics of the collectivists, from what Aristophanes
had been saying in Athens in 400 B.C.

II

There has, nevertheless, been a tremendous increase during
the past two centuries in the efficacy, the unceasing impact, and
the deadliness of the collectivist weapons. It is the basic reason
for this huge difference that is the chief theme of our concern
tonight. And that difference can be expressed quite simply in
just one word: *organization*. Under Pisistratus during the early
part of the sixth century B.C., or under Cleisthenes at the end of
that century, the use of the hypocrisies and agitations of class
struggle by those men to establish and maintain themselves in
power was a recurrent but disconnected and more or less hap-
hazard manifestation of mere personal opportunism. The forces
of evil were continuous, but the continuity of their collectivist
activities was not maintained by any organizations transcending
the lives of individual tyrants. Even up to the time of Pericles,
the strongly collectivist measures of this ruler were carried out
with full lip service being paid to the freedom of individuals,
and on the supposedly immediate consent, rather than any vested
consent, by those being governed to the mushrooming of the
functions of government. Under these circumstances, and because Pericles dedicated to such worthy causes that increasing
part of the labor and productivity of the Athenians which was
appropriated by government, the alignment of the forces of evil
on the collectivist side and of the forces of good on the individualistic side became far less clear-cut under his regime than they
had been under earlier tyrants or were soon to become again.

AND A SOLIDIFYING OF THE LEFT . . .

But by this time, in Sparta a whole new psychological factor had been brought into the struggle. This was a collectivist tyranny that was self-perpetuating through whichever oligarchic rulers might successively wield the power of government; which collectivist tyranny brazenly claimed the vested right and did exercise the continuing power to absorb all privileges and all responsibilities into the hands of government, doling out to individuals only such narrowly restricted areas of personal freedom as the government chose to grant. No longer did a collectivist tyranny die, at least temporarily, with a particular tyrant. No longer did the collectivist forces of evil have to roll with the punch at each new *interregnum* between their agents until their concerted force could be rallied again behind some strongman opportunist of sufficient ruthlessness and cunning. The control by these forces of the instrumentalities of government power and of all the brutalizing, stultifying, destructive mechanics and propaganda of collectivism was now continuous from one generation to the next. For the forces of individualism to reassert themselves, not just the ephemeral power of a single tyrant but the entrenched power of the whole Spartan system had to be overthrown. And this factor of continuity and organization was of sufficient importance to enable Sparta through two generations of mixed cold war and hot war to conquer the Greek world, and to keep its collectivist tyranny imposed on this whole Greek world, including Athens, for yet another full generation.

In fact the pattern for all future completely totalitarian collectivist regimes was so well established by fascist Sparta that there is only one major difference between its basic philosophy and that of our Soviet enemies today. And the economic and political organization of the Spartan state, as well as the methods of infiltration and subversion which it used for gradual conquests of the whole Greek world, were so similar to those of Soviet

Russia as to astound anybody who studies this subject for the first time.

But the Spartan tyranny was eventually overthrown. Before any new clique of collectivist brutalizers could establish themselves with a continuous organization in power, Alexander the Great had brought Greece under the sway of a worldwide despotism with the frankly oriental concept that governmental powers derived not from the counting of oyster shells but from the sweep of the sword. And by the time his empire fell to pieces Rome was introducing a whole new era, and in many respects a whole new civilization, to the pages of man's history. So that Sparta remained as an example to be followed, a goal to be sought, and an experience from which to profit on the part of collectivists of later centuries. But it did not establish an esoteric core of uninterrupted organizational permanence to control and guide collectivist drives for power in the centuries ahead.

The precedent had been set, however, and the vision obviously reoccurred to many evil men during those two thousand years. There were many small sects and heresies and societies and associations of which we catch fleeting glimpses now and then from the early centuries of the Christian era until they proliferated into numerous clumps of unsightly or even poisonous intellectual weeds after 1700. How many of them there were, each of which intended to be the embryo of an organization that would grow in power until it ruled the world, we do not know. How many revolutionary coups or insurrections, or how many more gradual and more peaceful impositions of tyrannical power by ambitious criminals mouthing the hypocrises of collectivism, may have been "masterminded" by such esoteric groups, we do not know. How extensive or long lasting was the once well-established cult of Satanism, which incorporated into its beliefs, methods, and purposes practically all of the foulness now associated with our contemporary tyranny, Communism, we do not know. For a high degree of secrecy was not only essential to any even temporary success on the part of any of these nefarious collections of criminal con men, but the thrill of belonging to some mysterious and powerful inner circle was one of the strongest appeals any such group could offer to prospective recruits.

We do know, however, from hundreds of small leaks and published accounts that the doctrines which gave many of these secret groups their cohesiveness and continuity would fall clearly, and by the most tolerant classification, into the category of evil. Also, that by the eighteenth century A.D. these various doctrines had pretty much coalesced into a uniformly Satanic creed and program, which was to establish the power of the sect through the destruction of all governments, all religion, all morality, all economic systems; and to substitute the sheer physical force of the lash and the bayonet for all other means by which previous governments, good or bad, had contrived to rule mankind. And a most important one of these groups, which is now generally meant when we use the term *Illuminati*—although many others had called themselves by that same name—was founded on May 1, 1776, by Adam Weishaupt.

Eventually Gives Birth to the Modern Monster . . .

Despite the extreme secrecy with which this group cloaked itself from the very beginning, one early raid by the Bavarian government, another raid about three years later, the partial confessions at one arraignment of four men fairly high up in the conspiracy—all of whom, incidentally, were professors— and a few more or less accidental discoveries or disclosures from other sources have made the original nature, purposes, and methods of the *Illuminati* quite well known. Since by 1800 they were able to pull the veil of secrecy over themselves almost completely and permanently, we do not know to what extent Weishaupt's group became the central core or even one of the main components of a continuing organization with increasing reach and control over all collectivist activities after 1776. But that there have been one or more such organizations, which have now been absorbed into the top echelons of the Communist conspiracy—or vice versa—is supported by too much evidence of too many kinds to permit much doubt. Both because of the strong probability that Weishaupt's *Illuminati* has been the dominant factor in this development, therefore, and because if there has been some even more secret and more successful group to fill the role it is bound to have had an extreme degree of similarity to the Weishaupt clique, it is worthwhile for us to take a few paragraphs to examine some of the clearly established facts about this particular sect of *Illuminati*. For a mere recital of these facts will show, among other things, how inevitable is the conclusion that the present worldwide Communist conspiracy has evolved out of some such earlier organization.

There was published in 1798 a book which is now extremely rare, but of which I have a copy, in which 130 pages were devoted to exposure of the *Illuminati*. This consisted primarily of testimony and letters which had been made available through raids or investigations ordered by the elector of Bavaria. In the June 1962 issue of *American Opinion*, Dr. Revilo Oliver gave the substance of the information which had come to light through a raid in 1786 on the home of a high-ranking member named Zwack. From these several direct, primary, and contemporary sources, it is easy to assemble the following fully documented picture:

(1) Selected neophytes were brought into the order in the conviction that its general object was "the happiness of the human race." After about three years of receiving intensive instruction and observation as a novitiate—such lesser members were called Minervals—those selected to be taken further were given a fuller explanation. The aim of the order was "to make of the human race, without any distinction of nation, condition, or profession, one good and happy family." Does that sound familiar?

(2) By this time, also, the Minerval, if accepted to go on to becoming an *Illuminatus Minor*, was being taught that all

religion was merely superstition, which should be abandoned in favor of enlightenment—in other words, illumination—and the triumph of reason. One of the idealistic inducements which brought many recruits into the Order was the assurance that it would help to spread the purest and noblest form of Christianity. Many Protestant ministers, during the initial three years of brainwashing to which they were subjected, then actually came to equate the doctrines and purposes of the Order with the purest form of Christianity, and were ready to shift their allegiance to the worship of *reason* by the time they were called upon to do so.

(3) Loyalty to the temporal powers of the time was solemnly promised by the Order, and was understood by new members to be a firm principle of the Order when they took the oath as Minervals. By the time one came, however, to take the far more serious oath as an *Illuminatus Minor*, he was already accepting the doctrine that the happiness of the human race required the uniting of all the inhabitants of the earth into one great family; that the abolition of national differences and animosities being requisite to this end, patriotism was a narrow-minded sentiment incompatible with the more enlarged views and purposes of the Order; and that consequently all ruling princes were to be regarded as unnecessary and expendable. Loyalty to the Order was represented as morally far superior to loyalty to the ruling powers.

One passage in Weishaupt's own explanation of the oath required at this point in a member's progress—given in a letter which he certainly never intended should be made public—is so revealing as to merit quoting in full:

These [ruling] powers are despots when they do not conduct themselves by its [that is, the Order's] principles; and it is therefore our duty to surround them with its members, so that the profane may have no access to them. Thus we are most powerfully to promote its [the Order's] interests. If any person is more disposed to listen to Princes than to the Order, he is not fit for it, and must rise no higher. We must do our utmost to procure the advancement of *Illuminati* into all important civil offices.

As a corollary to these instructions, it is to be noted, Weis-haupt's *Illuminati* contrived to place their members as tutors to youths of great rank or importance. They managed by in-fluence and intrigue to get dignitaries favorable to themselves appointed to higher offices. And the diligence and skill with which they worked at promoting each other is illustrated by the fact that within a comparatively few years all of the chairs at Weishaupt's own University of Ingolstadt, with two excep-tions, were occupied by *Illuminati*. When you thus realize that the Communists today may have had a hundred and fifty years of cumulative experience at these tricks, you cease to marvel at what they accomplish with such comparatively small numbers.

(4) Sensual pleasures were to be given high rank among those to be pursued for the happiness of mankind. This was gradually to be made clear to the Minervals; and the release by enlighten-ment or "illumination" of the restrictions on such pleasures, as formerly imposed by their consciences, was to be one of the subconscious appeals leading them to the worship of reason in-stead of religion. And any similarity of this process to the motivations which have produced the disgusting beatniks of both sexes that now overrun Harvard Square may not be at all co-incidental.

(5) Nothing was more insistently and repeatedly emphasized on members than the propriety of employing, for a good pur-pose, the means which the wicked employed for evil purposes. It was taught that the preponderance of good (that is, good from the Order's point of view) in the ultimate result of any action to be considered made any means justifiable; and that wisdom and virtue consisted of properly determining this bal-ance with regard to any situation. More specifically, nothing was to be scrupled at by a member if the superiors of the mem-ber could make it appear that the Order would derive advan-tage from it, because the great objective of the Order was su-perior to all other considerations.

(6) The method of education of the Minervals was intended to make them and all members of the society spies on all other

members. One of the most important activities of a Minerval by which he was judged as to whether he should be advanced to the next level consisted of the sealed reports he was required to turn in to superiors he had never seen on the methods and efficiency and views of the immediate superior who was giving him his three years of instructions.

(7) Keeping secret all of the activities of the Order, and even its very existence, was stressed at all times as of the utmost importance. And dire vengeance was promised any member who ever betrayed its secrets, even if he had been dismissed or for any other reason had ceased to be a member.

(8) Self-criticisms by a member of his own failures and shortcomings, especially with regard to his conduct on any occasions where he himself had doubts as to its propriety or wisdom, were required by his superiors. And such reports or confessions were to include some account of his friendships *and of his unorthodox opinions*, as well as of his conduct, on such occasions.

(9) The most important of all knowledge for a member to acquire was an understanding of human character and motivations. For only thus would he be able to bend those with whom he came in contact to the service of the Order's purposes.

(10) The baneful influence of accumulated property was declared to be an insurmountable obstacle to the happiness of any nation. Although the Order chose by preference to recruit from the younger sons of important families who might be encouraged to resentment against the results of the rules of primogeniture, the full impact of this principle of the society with regard to property was not made clear until the Minerval progressed to the point of taking his oath as an *Illuminatus Minor*. At that time, this long and solemn oath included the following:

I bind myself to perpetual silence and unshaken loyalty and submission to the Order, in the persons of my Superiors; here making a faithful and complete surrender of my private judgment, my own will, and every narrow-minded employment of my power and influence. I pledge myself to account the good of the Order as my own, and am ready to serve it with my fortune, my honor, and my blood. Should I, through omission, neglect, passion, or wickedness, behave contrary to the good of the Order, I subject myself to what reproof or punishment my Superiors shall enjoin.

AND THE MONSTROUS REALITY BEGINS TO EMERGE . . .

All of the above, and a great deal more, the Minerval had learned and promised by the time he really became a fully accepted member of the Order. The training, the disillusionment, the gradual acceptance of the real purposes of the Order continued until one who was properly qualified became at last a member of the inner circle. By that time the following facts had been made crystal clear to him, and he was a party to all that they signified:

A. The purpose of the Order was to rule the world.

B. In order to accomplish this, it would first be necessary to destroy contemporary civilization. This specifically included the overthrow of all existing governments; the merging of all nationalities and races into one people under one government; the abolition of all private property; the destruction of all religion; and the abrogation of all morality.

C. Any and all means were to be used to achieve this end. Whatever helped the Order was good, whatever hindered it was bad.

D. A philosophical front glorifying equality, and a new kind of "morality" were to be utilized wherever they would serve. The essence of the "morality" was that the world should come to be ruled only by able men and good men, in all positions and at all levels. But the important and undisclosed catch was that who qualified as good men and able men was to be determined solely by the Order.

E. Any and all persons, of whatever rank or character, who could forward the purposes of the Order in any way were to be utilized as much as possible, without any necessity for them to be members and perhaps without their even knowing of the Order's existence.

F. This incredibly ambitious undertaking was to be conducted as a conspiracy, and secrecy at every point and at all times was of utmost importance.

UGLY AND RUTHLESS . . .

One or two somewhat incidental comments seem to be worth the space before we move on. It was made a custom from the very beginning to identify European cities by names taken from classical geography, and for those high enough up in the Order to choose a fictitious name by which they would always be identified, in correspondence or otherwise, to other members of the inner circle. Cato, Marius, Brutus, Pythagoras, Socrates, Hannibal, were typical of the names selected. Weishaupt, head of the Order, called himself Spartacus—for the man who led the most famous slave revolt in Roman history. May we be pardoned for a mild speculation as to whether this accounts in some degree, directly or indirectly, for the great current veneration for the slave leader Spartacus in the mind of so many liberals.

Second, the important leaders of the *Illuminati* practiced what they preached with regard to morality. They were liars and scoundrels and embezzlers and debauchers all—in their personal lives, as well as in the line of duty. One of the great concerns of Spartacus, popping up here and there in the very correspondence which was uncovered, was how to have Cato's sister murdered in order to prevent the public learning that he (Weishaupt-Spartacus) had seduced her; and that his attempts to have the secret buried by an abortion had failed. His justification for the desired murder was that the damage which these disclosures might do to *his* reputation would be harmful to the Order!

And yet, right while this little problem was perplexing him, Spartacus wrote to Cato (who obviously knew nothing of his sister's seduction) as follows:

What shall I do? I am deprived of all help. Socrates, who would insist on being a man of consequence among us, and is really a man of talents, *and of a right way of thinking*, is eternally besotted. Augustus is in the worst estimation imaginable. Alcibiades sits the day long with the vintner's pretty wife, and there he sighs and pines. A few days ago, at Corinth [we do not know the actual city meant —RW], Tiberius attempted to ravish the wife of Democides and her husband came in upon them. Good heavens! What *Areopagitae* I have got. When the worthy man Marcus Aurelius [an extremely influential prospective recruit—RW] comes to Athens [Munich] what will he think? What a meeting with dissolute immoral wretches, whoremasters, liars, bankrupts, braggarts, and vain fools! When he sees all this, what will he think? He will be ashamed to enter into an Association where the chiefs raise the highest expectations, and exhibit such a wretched example; and all this from self-will, from sensuality. . . . We may sacrifice to the Order our health, our fortune, and our reputation [!!] and these Lords, following their own pleasures, will whore, cheat, steal, and drive on like shameless rascals; and yet must be *Areopagitae*, and interfere in everything.

Alas, poor Spartacus. Our heart bleeds for him in his perplexity, so frankly and virtuously expressed in this letter to one whom he addresses as his "dearest friend." But of just such men as he describes, and even worse, have the top councils of the collectivist forces of evil been composed from the days of the Gracchi to those of Khrushchev, Tito, Castro, and Sukarno— and of some even closer to home.

It is not our duty nor our need tonight to explore the extent to which the *Illuminati* were responsible for, or contributed to, bringing on the French Revolution with all of its excesses and reign of terror. The evidence increases that their influence was powerful and extensive. More important, if there were time, would be a discussion of the methods used, especially to excite and manipulate the Paris mobs—on which mobs the successful destructiveness wreaked on the state, on religion, and on all morality depended. All was lies, planned agitation and mob action, murders carefully plotted to appear as spontaneous "vengeance" by the people, incredible terror used as a political weapon—all in the name of reason and of liberty, equality, and brotherhood.

FOR EXAMPLE . . .

Let's spare a paragraph to talk about the Bastille as just one illustration. This ancient prison was of little concern to the populace of Paris in 1789. It had originally been a place of incarceration, not for ordinary people like themselves, but for prisoners of high rank. It had now fallen largely into disuse even for that purpose, and had become at the worst a reminder of bygone tyranny. The dungeons had been in disuse for a quarter of a century. The rooms that were still used for prisoners of any kind were comfortably furnished and the food was "excellent and plentiful." And there was a movement already under foot to have the old prison torn down by the government itself and replaced with a public square.

It took tremendous effort and expense, and a lot of cunning and planning, on the part of the revolutionary leaders (some of whom, at least, are known to have been *Illuminati*) to foment the march of a huge mob on the Bastille and make its capture look like the spontaneous action of an outraged people. It required more planning and more organizational skill than was recently dedicated by Bayard Rustin to his "spontaneous" march on Washington of his grossly exaggerated hundreds of thousands of "civil rights" agitators. The purpose for which most of the French mob actually marched on the Bastille was to get arms, which the conspirators had convinced them they could seize there and would need—because of other disorders throughout the city that had been plotted and instigated by these same conspirators. A much smaller crowd, already armed and led by actual revolutionaries, arrived on the scene after the big mob had assembled. We'll not go into all of the acts of arson, trickery, and provocation practiced by this armed crowd on a humanitarian governor, who was simply trying to save lives and still do his duty, before the point was reached when the now thoroughly excited large mob attained entrance to and stormed through the castle. But that most ardent of revolutionaries, Jean Paul Marat, is himself the authority for this statement of what really happened.

"The Bastille," he wrote, "ill defended, was taken by a few soldiers and a troop of wretches, mostly Germans and also provincials. The Parisians—those eternal idlers—appeared at the fortress but curiosity alone brought them there to visit the dark dungeons, of which the mere idea froze them with terror." But the butcheries perpetrated by the combined mob, once it overflowed the fortress, on the loyal governor and the faithful old guards, and on many brave men who tried to bring order and sense out of the instigated frenzy, were something to make the whole human race blush with shame and cry with compassion.

As to the horribly mistreated prisoners, the mob found but seven inmates altogether in the whole Bastille, living quite comfortably. Four were forgers, two were lunatics who had been mad before they were imprisoned, and one was a count who had been incarcerated for "monstrous crimes" at the request of his family. In the chaos and confusion the four forgers simply disappeared. The two lunatics eventually wound up in the asylum at Charenton. And the count was returned to his disappointed relatives. The mob found no captives in chains, no skeletons nor corpses, no torture chambers, and none of the horrors it had been excitedly led to expect. The terror and the horror were entirely and only those perpetrated by the mob itself.

This is the greatly softened and far too briefly told but real story of the siege and fall of the Bastille. Yet that event, in line with the propaganda and methods of the collectivist criminals of all ages, has been glorified to this day as a great noble act of the people in search of liberty. Its date, July 14, is still honored as the national holiday of France. Most of you were taught in your history book—and few of you, I suspect, have ever taken the trouble to learn otherwise—that this was one of the glorious events of all history. As some informed writer has stated: "A new era was born of a prodigious lie. Liberty bore a stain from its birth, and the paradox once created can never be dispelled."

The further truth is that the French people under Louis XVI had as little cause to let themselves be led by conspiratorial destructivists into insane horrors and a murderous clamor for "liberty" as the Negroes in America have today in a demand for "freedom." Both are being stirred and led into the same kind of cruel idiocy by exactly the same kind of revolutionary criminals, for exactly the same megalomaniacal purposes on the part of the real instigators of these monstrous crimes against God and country. If the march on Washington had been more successful from the point of view of the Communists; if the common sense and basic morality of the American people—white and black—had already been sufficiently eroded by Communist wiles and propaganda so that the marchers could have been whipped up into the same kind of frenzy as were a smaller contingent of three hundred such marchers recently in the city of Chester, Pennsylvania; and if carefully planted armed goons of the Communists within the ranks of the marchers on Washington could have arranged for the burning of the city, and for murders and atrocities to be perpetrated on a number of loyal congressmen and senators, all to look like the spontaneous actions of an infuriated, resentful mob seeking freedom, then you might easily have seen the date of *that* great lie established in due course as the new national holiday of a "liberated" United States. And at least you would have seen an almost exact parallel to the sack of the Bastille.

OF WORSE TO COME . . .

The French Revolution turned out to be, in fact, a rehearsal in almost every particular of what the whole world is facing today. Compressed into one city and a period of six years, 1789 through 1794, were all of the lies and crimes and horror and propaganda and destructiveness which are now being applied to the whole world over a period of about six decades.

Whether the top command of the international Communist conspiracy is simply a continuing part of Weishaupt's *Illuminati*

under whatever names and in whatever forms it may have perpetuated itself, we do not know. As Dr. Oliver has pointed out,
we do know that Karl Marx wrote the *Communist Manifesto*
in 1847 simply as an agent employed by one such group, the
so-called League of Just Men, which already had branches in
many countries long before it was renamed as the League of
Communists. My own lesser researches clearly indicate that the
infamous so-called German Union, and other revolutionary bodies with exactly the same purposes and methods as the *Illuminati*,
which helped the identified Weishaupt *Illuminati* mightily in
bringing on the French Revolution, were nothing more or less
than divisions or branches of the *Illuminati* which had been set
up separately for purposes of deception, protection and convenience. It could easily be that the League of Just Men was
just a division of the *Illuminati*; that Karl Marx and, after him,
Trotsky and Lenin and Stalin and Malenkov, and de Gaulle and
Castro and Nehru and Betancourt, and hundreds of other leftist
leaders elsewhere throughout the world, and a dozen in this
country whom we had better leave unnamed, have all been
working for such an inner group, or in some cases, have been
members of it.

We do not know. For most purposes and in most respects it
does not matter enough to deserve more than passing attention
or speculation. What does matter, and the point to which this
whole speech has been leading so far, is that forces of evil, which
work through collectivism, are always organized; while the opposing forces of good, which support and defend the rights and
responsibilities of individuals, are always disorganized. And this
seems to me the primary reason, above all other reasons, why it
sometimes takes so long for the forces of good, with all truth on
their side, to come out from under the slavery or suppression or
ignominy to which they are recurrently subjected for a generation or a century by the forces of evil.

Throughout all of the history which we reviewed so briefly at
the beginning of this talk, the forces of evil have been organized

for every fray; the forces of good have never been organized except during those last-ditch, often suicidal, but sometimes successful spasms of effort to throw off a collectivist tyranny, when enough individuals had finally come to recognize it as unbearable. And now we face an extension of this principle which makes it tremendously more important. For in our contemporary world the forces of evil are not only more elaborately and tightly and lastingly organized than ever before; and not only do they have the benefit of an organization which has visibly been continuous and growing for many decades; but whether or not this organization is merely a continuation of one which has been active for nearly two hundred years, it has obviously taken full and remarkable advantage of the accumulated knowledge and experience of collectivist groups which *have* been active throughout that period.

The Communist party of Khrushchev does not have to be a direct organizational descendant of Weishaupt's *Illuminati* to be able to benefit from everything the collectivists learned from their manipulation and use of that incredibly slimy hypocrite Mirabeau, or of the equally nauseating though far less brilliant traitor the duc d'Orleans, in steering the French Revolution onto the course they had designed. The very fact that both Mirabeau and the duc d'Orleans were members of the *Illuminati*, although not trusted members and only half-illuminated—and hence to be treated as members only as long as they were useful and then tossed to the wolves—these and many other such experiences and accomplishments of Weishaupt and his inner circle can supply the top Communist command today with many guidelines as to how to deal with a Ngo dinh Diem or a Juan Bosch or a João Goulart or a Juan Peron. While the anti-Communists of the world simply do not have, and never have had, any organizational continuity which gives the slightest chance of their even learning about, and much less utilizing, the experiences from past encounters which are repeated over and over.

TILL ENTERS THE JOHN BIRCH SOCIETY . . .

As one of my associates has said, the Communists have missed *nothing*, absolutely nothing, among all the possibilities for deception, propaganda, and aggression in any and all situations which may arise. While the anti-Communists appear to have learned absolutely nothing from the past. I have never seen an anti-Communist who even recognized the similarities between the characters, careers, and utterly false historical legends of Cornelia, the mother of the Gracchi, and of Eleanor Roosevelt. I have never seen one that recognized in Alcibiades such an instructive prototype of Dwight D. Eisenhower. I have never seen one who pointed out the unbelievably numerous and extensive parallels between the Spartan state during the Peloponnesian War and the USSR during the war we are fighting today.

But the Communists obviously learned directly from the story of Sparta, or from organizations which have passed this knowledge on to the contemporary Communists, that the family must be weakened and then destroyed as a sociological unit by any totalitarian collectivist regime. And it is the very fact that the individualists will learn nothing from history, have no organizational means or opportunity of learning anything from history, which so helps the collectivists to perpetrate repetitions of tragic history on us again and again. All of which discussion and background leads us, as you are certain to have been surmising, to The John Birch Society. For we feel that it is clearly our duty, and may be our destiny, to fill this void. And bringing out what we mean in this connection will give me an opportunity to repeat, clarify, or emphasize two or three other basic principles and purposes of the Society.

A. In the last pages of the Blue Book, as simply a transcript of what was said at the founding meeting of The John Birch Society, it is pointed out that I think we are something new in history. I still think so, and this speech has been intended partly to explain and support the thought. Because this is the first time in history, so far as we know, that any sizable group of truly good men and women of all religious beliefs, and of all races and colors, has ever been brought together in any permanent voluntary organization to work, as a group, for those things which they believe in common.

There are several basic reasons why this kind of association has never been achieved before. The first is that good men and women are, necessarily, those who believe in the responsibility of the individual; who are, therefore, individualistic in their thinking. They instinctively realize the truth of Kipling's lines that "the ill ye do by two and two, ye must pay for one by one," and that the individual can take credit only for his own good deeds and not for those of the crowd. As individualists, the truly good men and women are reluctant to merge themselves into any secular body where close ties with others, who may have divergent views, might call for defenses or compromises of their own beliefs. But we have overcome that obstacle by our insistence that we do not even want men and women whose characters and personal beliefs have rounded edges. The whole key to our working together is tolerance, not compromise.

As a Voluntary Group of Individualists . . .

We must agree basically on morality, integrity, and purpose; and on the fundamental goals of the Society, which are less government, more responsibility, and a better world. Otherwise there would be no point in our coming together, and there is no reason for anybody not subscribing to those principles to join our great undertaking. But it is obvious today that there are enough people who agree with these basic principles, and with our organizational plans for their support, to make of The John Birch Society a permanent and growing body; one in which the forces of good can maintain a lasting union and a continuing concerted effort. We believe, therefore, as already stated, that for this reason and in this manner The John Birch Society can become a new force in human history—one that has been very badly needed, especially for the past two hundred years; and that, as such a new force, it can become a very effective factor on the side of the forces of good in making this a better world. For at least not *all* of the advantages of organization and of continuity will now be left on the side of the forces of evil.

B. Not all of the forces of evil, nor all evil men, use the tools or pressures of collectivism to serve their selfish purposes. The bank robber, the man who kills the husband of his mistress, the man who is such a liar that he develops the best memory in the county in order to keep up with his falsehoods—these may even be individualists. In fact, as a boy in Democratic North Carolina, I heard on reliable authority that horse thieves had even been known to vote the Republican ticket. And we regard bank robbers, murderers, liars and horse thieves as enemies of The John Birch Society; and, in fact, as enemies of all society, even if and when such criminals do happen to be conservatives with a strong penchant for *laissez-faire*.

So collectivism is not our only enemy. But we are permanently, eternally, and completely opposed to collectivism, as either political philosophy or as an activist conspiracy. On the contemporary scene we refer to the conspiratorial collectivists as Communists. Obviously we must stop these conspirators from gradually imposing their system on the rest of mankind, and we must rout the conspiracy, before we can move forward with our long-range constructive purposes. But the important point here is that we are also opposed to all collectivists, including the present-day Communists, even on the philosophical plane. For we seek less government, more responsibility, and a better world. The collectivists, on the other hand, are always and everywhere striving for more government and less individual responsibility. And the Communists today are also doing their utmost to bring about a completely amoral world.

In this fight on both levels, however, we have a twofold job. One is simply to carry on a continuous and increasingly large-scale educational program. Even for our now raging fight against the Communists, education is our basic strategy and truth is our only weapon. Did it ever occur to you to wonder why, with The John Birch Society no larger than it is, and having absolutely no official standing or support, the Communist periodicals in Moscow—which lay down the line for the Communists everywhere else to follow—have devoted more space to smearing The John Birch Society than they have ever given to any other non-official enemy in the whole forty years of their lying propaganda?

Well, I can tell you many reasons, but one most important reason. It is that we offer a new kind of opposition. Nowhere else, in any of the fifty countries the Communists have already taken over, have they ever had to contend with a sizable organization of patriots which was dedicated simply to the principle of bringing out the truth. The Communists do not fear arms or armies. In most of the world—even the so-called remaining free world—they control too many of the men who might give the order to march. They do not fear the bombs and missiles of push-button warfare. In most cases they now own the men who would have to push the buttons.

They do not fear purely political action. In every country they have proved their ability under all circumstances to control and stultify purely political action and mold it to their purposes.

But the Communists seek to impose and maintain their tyranny in any country with only about three percent of that country's population. Obviously this could not be done if even fifty percent of the population understood what was happening. All it would take to stop and rout the Communists in our own country completely in three months would be for enough Americans to become aware of what the Communists are doing, and how they are doing it. The necessary political action, through impeachments, through votes in Congress, through the actions of state legislatures and governors, through elections at every level, would follow so fast it would make your heads swim—and would make the Communists put their tails between their legs and scamper to their kennels. And of course the Communists know it. I only wish even our own members knew it half so well.

WE OFFER PERMANENT OPPOSITION TO COLLECTIVISM . . .

So it is our aim to become a huge and deeply dedicated educational army. But we also have a second task on which the first one and many opportunities and events in the future will all depend. That is simply to establish and maintain ourselves as a continuing organization of unshakable loyalty to the principles for which our great body came into existence. We shall thus be on hand as a rallying point whenever the collectivists arrive at one of those pages of future history where the weakness of good men and the parallel strength of organized evil men combine to give these forces of evil an opportunity to come out on top once again.

Let's make this whole thought clearer by specific illustrations. I most emphatically believe that if there had been in Athens during the fifth century B.C. a John Birch Society of just its present size, all Greece would have been spared the destructive horrors of the Peloponnesian Wars. I am equally certain that had there been in western Europe during all of the last half of the eighteenth century a John Birch Society of just its present dedicated strength, France would have been spared the six-year brutalizing terror and cruelties of the French Revolution. But there simply was *no* permanent, organized, continuing force in either instance to expose or offset the lies and pretenses and agitation of the contemporary versions of our present-day Communists.

On the current scene today the collectivist forces of evil are incredibly more extensive, more tightly organized, more experienced, more skillfully directed, and more solidly entrenched than they were in either Greece or western Europe right up to the actual holocaust of either time and place. So we are well aware that The John Birch Society has to become a great deal larger and stronger, *and to do so fast,* if we are to help decisively in preventing an exactly similar holocaust from engulfing our own country. But this does not alter the value of our concept. It merely makes us lament that The John Birch Society was not founded thirty years sooner; and it makes us more determined in our effort to catch up to the need.

C. Both for the present colossal battle, however, and for the long struggles ahead, we must keep our basic approach and objectives of a constructive nature. This doesn't mean any lack of defensive, preventive, or curative action against the Communist infection, or against the whole disease of collectivism. When a physician cuts out a tumor, or prevents smallpox by vaccination, his particular action may be negative or defensive, but it is certainly part of a constructive activity and purpose. Communism today, far from being any "wave of the future," is simply a huge dirty boil on the body of mankind. Like any boil it is very painful, and it is seeping poisons all through the body. It badly needs to be lanced and drained, so that the whole body can be restored to normal health with as small a permanent scar and as few lasting effects as possible. The concern of the doctor, when lancing and draining a boil, is the health of the body which has become infected. But a good physician will also do all he can to insist on cleanliness and proper living to prevent boils and to make the body of his patient more healthy —both before and after cutting out or curing any particular result of unhealthy living. And the analogy holds all the way for ourselves in doing our part as a physician towards giving the whole body of mankind a healthier mind in a healthier body.

It is this imperative need for positive, aggressive, constructive thinking and action and purpose which is the real theme of all I am saying to you tonight.

BY CONSTRUCTIVE MEANS . . .

In the Blue Book five years ago—it was on page 122 [page 114 in the paperbound edition]—I stated my conviction that we could never win even the immediate current battle with the

Communists "unless the promise of what we can build supplies more motivation than the terror of what we must destroy." And this speech has been prepared primarily to reemphasize that conviction. All of the rest of it has been intended as prelude to these final paragraphs. And the easiest way to make their purport clear is to look once again at the present battle from several specific viewpoints.

First, the Communists have been striving for the past fifty years to destroy, utterly and permanently, the three basic human loyalties. These are loyalty to God, loyalty to country, and loyalty to family. They simply must do so in order to become and remain victorious, for no permanent and completely totalitarian regime could possibly permit any loyalty other than to itself.

While the Communists' intended destruction of all religion is under way, they make as much use as they can of the organizational structure of religious bodies as a means of reaching large numbers of good men and women with subtle propaganda most favorably presented. They infiltrate the clergy of various denominations. Our job, however, is not just to expose and defend against this propaganda and infiltration, but to make the impact of real religion on our national life even stronger. Put in the broadest and most comprehensive language, we must counter all of the blasphemy, apostasy, and sacrilege being promoted around us by doing our part to "let more of reverence in us dwell." And within that broad purpose, we need in our own lives to make our own personal religious beliefs into closer, firmer guides for our actions and our consciences. And may I say that in all of these respects our members are doing wonderfully well indeed. Among the greatest encouragements that we constantly find on the quite rough road we are now traveling are the hundreds of letters from our Catholic, Protestant, and Jewish members alike, telling us that their work in, dedication to, and understanding of, The John Birch Society has caused their religion to come to mean more to them than ever before.

As to patriotism, everybody who could tell Khrushchev from

Smokey the Bear knows how intrinsically imperative a feature of Communism is its completely international structure and character. Despite the Communists' use of a flamboyant new pseudo-nationalism in formerly colonial areas during the transition period while a Ghana or a North Vietnam or a Congo is being converted from a British, French, or Belgian colony into a Soviet colony; and despite a few recurrent and very useful feuds based on the fraud of nationalistic divisions within the Communist family; nevertheless it is perfectly obvious that the Communists *must* do everything they can to destroy all real patriotic sentiment as rapidly as possible.

We need to counter this drive not just by defending our *independence* from subtle attempts to convert the very phrase into *interdependence,* and from all efforts to merge our nation into a one-world tyranny. And remember that the last two presidents of the United States used the Fourth of July, of all days, for speeches in praise of American *interdependence* with other nations. So the need here is great. But we must also seek at all times and everywhere to make our fellow citizens constantly more aware of the material, political, and spiritual accomplishments of our nation; of the greatness of its heroes; of its once glorious promise as the last best hope of man; and of the tremendous destiny that still awaits it as both a physical and a spiritual leader among the nations of the future. We must be willing not only to die for our country if that ultimate need arises, and in accordance with a noble tradition of mankind which the Communists have not yet been able to uproot; but we need to live for our country to the extent that the example and the produce of our daily lives can contribute to its greatness as a home for ourselves, our children, and their descendants.

INCLUDING POLITICAL ACTION . . .

All of which makes this a fitting place for just a word about politics. Clearly, as good citizens in a great country, where it is still theoretically and legally possible to make those who govern us responsible to the will of the governed, we must ourselves live up to the responsibility which that privilege imposes. Our policy, therefore, must not be to eschew political campaigns and political action at all, but simply to make them more fruitful and more worthwhile. We should use the wonderful opportunities offered by a political campaign as a means of enlightening ourselves and our fellow citizens on the issues and the leadership that are determining our future; and we should do all we can to see that candidates make full use of that same opportunity. The Society itself, for obvious reasons, can take no official part or position in any partisan political campaign. But our members should not only take part; they should, by both their example and their labors, raise the whole level of political campaigns to their proper place in the kind of republic our founding fathers tried to have us inherit and maintain.

As to family loyalties, the Communists are hacking away at this obstacle to their tyranny by every conceivable means from the eroding propaganda of television, stage, and screen to the examples being set by topflight national leaders who count on Communist support. The direction of their effort is shown by what they have been able to accomplish in Russia. There the child does not look to his parents, nor feel any gratitude to his parents, for the food he eats, the clothes he wears, the room in which he lives, the education he receives, or the pleasures and entertainments he is allowed. He looks solely to the state as the provider of all of these blessings. The transference of loyalty there is begun early; and it is made as complete as practical and political considerations will yet permit. And parallel to this movement, of course, has been a destruction of the sanctity of marriage, and of as many as possible of the countless ties that bind the family together as a sociological unit.

Now it is in the family circle that the feminine half of mankind's basic partnership justly earns credit for so large a part in human progress. The day-after-day influence of the mother in the family, through the exercise of love and patience and discipline and understanding, and through the inculcation into the children of ambition and generosity and a moral code and a sense of responsibility; it is this composite influence of all the mothers of any generation which has tremendous bearing on the position and the direction of the next generation. Goethe says: *Ewig-Weibliche zieht uns hinan* ("The eternal woman draws us on"). And it is certainly through the family that the eternal feminine makes *its* greatest contribution to the upward reach of all mankind.

Here again, it is not only our duty to resist the whole collectivist drive to destroy the family and to establish government *in loco parentis*. We must not only defend the family ideal against all of the pressures and propaganda which would destroy it, but we must strengthen that ideal and increase still further the ties and loyalties that make family units the very bricks out of which a stable and happy society is built.

AND A THOUSAND SPECIFIC EFFORTS . . .

And now, solely for the sake of making our meaning clearer, let's turn for illustrations to more particular points of dispute between the collectivists and ourselves on the immense front where the present battle lines are drawn. Let us remember that many of the objectives, little or large, are not possible today— and most of them will not be easy at any time. These are ends to be sought and opportunities to be seized through an unceasing remembrance of our larger goals of which they are comparatively small components; they are not assignments for which you punch a time clock every morning.

It is not enough for us to try to prevent the further expansion of government. We must constantly try to reduce the size of the governments that we have. For the whole key to the problem of government is not in its character nor in its form, but in its quantity. There is simply no way in which you can make *big* government, *extensive* government, behave. The only way to accomplish the desired result is also the simplest way. Keep government or reduce government to the absolute minimun.

So this is one reason, of course, why we should give a round of applause to the promoters of the Liberty Amendment. For there you have a determined, single-purpose drive to reduce the size of government by removing some of the funds that support a profligate bureaucracy.

It is not enough for us to resist and condemn the deliberate inflation of our currency by government. We must fight for a return to a gold-backed, completely redeemable, *unmanaged* currency. And the most important word in that sentence is "unmanaged." Some years ago we published an article by Hans Sennholz, a very brilliant disciple of von Mises, on the "Federal Reserve System." Sennholz was aware, as are many in this audience today, but as most of the American people never have been, that the kind of control over money exercised through the Federal Reserve System was one of the cardinal planks in the whole Marxian program. Like the graduated income tax and other lesser parts of the same program, it was imposed on the American people by highly placed Marxian influences in the Woodrow Wilson administration. And Sennholz ended his compacted survey with the conclusion that, despite the very best of intentions on the part of a preponderant majority of all the officials of the system, without the Federal Reserve the United States could not be dragged into socialism, while with the Federal Reserve socialism could not be avoided.

A friend of mine sent a copy of this article to the head of one of the Federal Reserve banks. He in turn had an answer written by one of the bright young bureaucrats in his banking empire. And that answer began with this sentence: "Somebody has to manage money; it certainly will not manage itself." Which meant that the rest of the whole paper was only so much junk. Either unconsciously or deliberately the young expert had completely missed the whole point. For a managed currency is like a yardstick by which everything must be measured, but with the length of the yardstick itself being constantly changed by government. It is only to the extent that money is *not* made the tool of the value judgments or of the political ambitions or of the ideological purposes of the planners that it serves its basic purposes. It is only to the extent that money is *unmanaged*, and is a completely passive medium, that it becomes so useful a common denominator into which to convert and through which to exchange the infinite results of man's productivity and the measures of his desires. In fact, the freedom of money from *management* runs remarkably parallel throughout all history to the freedom of man himself from collectivist tyranny. And we must fight for both freedoms at every turn.

It is not enough for us to condemn the present increasing centralization of our schools, and the extension of that tendency into a drive for the federalization of all education. We must seek constantly to provide better local schools, and a better understanding of how much their advantages outweigh the loss of efficiency supposedly provided by centralization.

A decade ago a few very able industrialists, and an equal number of able educators, with myself as a very small fish in that pond, gathered repeatedly throughout two years in all-day meetings to hammer out a document which finally ran to thirty-two printed pages. But the whole core of that document to which we wanted the educators to agree and to which they did finally agree (much to their own amazement) was the statement that in America the education of youth is the ultimate responsibility of their parents; and that under the United States Constitution, the largest and highest government body which can thus act as an agency for the parents is a state government.

Despite all of the deliberately unconstitutional violations of that principle which we see around us today, it is just as sound now as it was then. And we should work at every opportunity to return all educational units and facilities to circumstances in which their responsiveness to the will of the parents is more significant and more obvious. We should also do all we can to restore among parents a conscious sense of their own responsibility for the education, training, and attitudes given to their children by the agencies to which they have delegated their own duties. For again all other freedoms, as best shown by the reverse illustrations of ancient Sparta and Soviet Russia today, run quite parallel to the extent that education can be kept diffused, decentralized, subject to the infinite small fluid errors of differing groups instead of the few huge petrified errors of centralized government; and can be kept free from the use of education by such a central power as a weapon of its tyranny.

FAR INTO THE FUTURE . . .

There are in my notes a dozen more illustrations of similar purport, taken from every division and activity of our national life. But at this point I was sure, simply in writing this speech, that the time had come to wind it up. So let's do so with despatch. In this warm war now, which is rapidly getting warmer, and in all of the cold wars, tepid wars, and even hot wars of the long future between the collectivist forces of evil and the individualistic forces of good, The John Birch Society must contribute organizational strength and firm leadership along the lines clearly indicated by our upward reach.

We must oppose secrecy with openhandedness. We must publish to the world our beliefs, our purposes, and our methods as fully as the collectivists conceal and disguise their own. We must oppose conspiracy, not with counter conspiracy, but with exposure, justice, and education. We must oppose falsehoods with truth; blasphemy with reverence; foul means with good means; immorality and amorality with more spiritual faith and dedication; rootlessness and chaos with tradition and stability; relativity with absolutes; pragmatism with deeper purposes; hedonism with a more responsible pursuit of happiness; cruelty with compassion; and hatred with love.

We must oppose the collectivists in every way, because both their methods and their purposes are diametrically contrary to our own. But above all we must oppose their willful destructiveness of all we have inherited with an equally strong and creative determination to improve and enrich that inheritance. We must be constant and conscious helpers in the building of more beautiful, more permanent, and more useful structures in the physical, the political, and the spiritual areas of association and joint effort with our fellowmen.

As is well known to some of you, I have much love for poetry. And I am not deterred in the least from quoting verses of the nineteenth century poets merely because they are ridiculed by the superficial sophisticates of today as didactic or commonplace or outmoded. The Ten Commandments and the Sermon on the Mount are the two most hackneyed pieces of literature in a score of languages, but they are still rated pretty high by several hundred million people. So let me try to wrap up our thought for this evening for you in a leading sequence of three or four extracts from some widely scattered poetic sermons of a century ago.

The first is from Tennyson, with a passing tribute to an earlier poet:

> I hold it truth with him who sings
> > To one clear harp in divers tones
> > That men may rise on stepping stones
> Of their dead selves to higher things.

And again from Tennyson:

> Men, my brothers, men the workers, ever reaping something new;
> That which they have done but earnest of the things that they
> > shall do.

Next from Cowper, who laments:

> > So slow
> The growth of what is excellent; so hard
> T'attain perfection in this nether world.

Which is answered—despite our knowledge that our progress in all ways and at all times is incomplete, stumbling, frequently thrown back, and must again be made over torn roads traveled before—which is still answered by the conviction of Whittier:

> Step by step since time began
> > I see the steady gain of man.

Then let's move on to a dream many of us have of a golden age to be achieved through more individual responsibilities, on higher tablelands of freedom than we have ever reached before. John Ruskin painted it for us:

Awake! Awake! the stars are pale, the east is russet gray;
They fade, behold the phantoms fade, that keep the gates of Day;
Throw wide the burning valves, and let the golden streets be free.
The morning watch is past—the watch of evening shall not be.

Put off, put off your mail, ye kings, and beat your brands to dust;
A surer grasp your hands must know, your hearts a better trust;
Nay, bend aback the lance's point, and break the helmet bar,—
A noise is on the morning winds; but not the noise of war!

For aye, the time of wrath is past, and near the time of rest,
And honor binds the brow of man, and faithfulness his breast,
Behold, the time of wrath is past, and righteousness shall be,
And the Wolf is dead in Arcady and the Dragon in the sea!

And at last we come to the exhortation of Dr. Holmes which served as our text and which we like to think of as applicable to our individual selves, to The John Birch Society, and indeed to all mankind.

Build thee more stately mansions, O my soul,
    As the swift seasons roll!
    Leave thy low-vaulted past!
Let each new temple, nobler than the last,
Shut thee from heaven with a dome more vast,
    Till thou at length are free,
Leaving thine outgrown shell by life's unresting sea!

Let me thank you, as earnestly as I can for such long, patient attention. And:

May God be with you till we meet again!

A Touch of Sanity

As first delivered at the West Los Angeles Veterans Memorial Building in Culver City, California, on March 9, 1965.

LADIES AND GENTLEMEN:

In 1860, when South Carolina was about to secede from the Union, one of its most distinguished statesmen, James L. Petigru, happened to be asked by a stranger the way to the Charleston insane asylum. He replied: "My dear Sir, take any road. You can't go wrong. The whole state is one vast insane asylum."

Well today, if anybody should, by some rare chance, ask you the way to an institution for the mentally deficient, your answer would require even less hesitation. "Mister," you could tell him, "don't budge an inch! You're not only in the middle of one, but you can't get out. Not only is the whole country now one vast insane asylum, but they are letting the worst patients run the place. And just about the only inmates they ever lock up any more are those that come nearest to being sane."

Now some of you may think I am exaggerating. And let's hope that I am. But before jumping to any conclusion, let's examine some of the evidence. Or, as an eminently sane American used to say, near the end of our more lucid era, "Let's look at the record." And we mean, let's look quite seriously at the proofs all around us that the American people as a whole are being led to act as if they had literally lost their senses.

II

We contend, for instance, that for our government to give millions of dollars of American money to Communist Poland, which Poland in turn and immediately gives to Ho chi Minh's Communist regime in North Vietnam, whom we are now fighting in South Vietnam—we say that this borders on insanity.

We contend that for the United States government to pay for the sending of bubble gum to Turkey, or Metrecal to Cambodia, or four million dollars worth of sex stimulants to Nationalist China, all under the guise of international development—well, we don't know exactly what it is they are supposed to be developing, but we say that all of this is close to insanity.

A year or more ago we saw by far the strongest nation on earth—our own—allow its citizens to be murdered in the Congo by a frenzied mob of Communist-inspired and Communist-controlled savages. Everything about the whole affair was planned and handled so as to reduce confidence in the United States and to increase fear of the Communists among the Africans.

The ultimate intention, of course, was to destroy the morale of the anti-Communists in Africa, and paralyze their will to resist. In the midst of these massacres our secretary of state, Dean Rusk, gave a tremendous boost to this Communist purpose by publicly begging the most bestial Communist viceroy in that part of the world, Jomo Kenyatta, to use *his* influence to save *our* citizens. Then we allowed our belated sending of planes to save some of our people to be presented by propaganda as meddling in the affairs of small nations. And the question was never even raised of demanding that the murdering savages be rounded up and tried for their crimes.

In Asia these demonstrations of utter and vicious contempt for the supposed power and trustworthiness of the United States have been referred to as "wringing the tail of the paper tiger," and have long played a most important part in the gradual surrender of that whole continent to the native Communist commissars anointed by Moscow. Now we have been seeing exactly the same formula at work in Africa. Any anti-Communist African leader, white or black, who is beguiled into putting the slightest trust in the ballyhooed and pretended opposition of Washington to Communism soon finds himself betrayed by Washington and destroyed by the logic of events. And we contend, Ladies and Gentlemen, that this course on the part of our government, in the circumstances that actually prevail in the world today, and in the light of past experience amounts to sheer insanity.

Or, let's look at a more serious and more immediate problem —the so-called war in Vietnam. Is it really a war, or isn't it? Nobody seems to know. We are told in one breath by the administration that it is simply a police action against guerillas within the boundaries of one country, South Vietnam; and hence that no declaration of war was feasible—for against whom would we declare it? But in the next breath the president himself proclaims that "this is war." And we read in our newspapers of bombing expeditions by our planes against various points in the supposedly independent country of North Vietnam; and about peace feelers to and from the government of that country.

But whether police action or war, under whose command is it being fought? The American people assume that since we are supplying all of the soldiers (except of course for the South Vietnamese themselves), and since we are paying all of the bills, this war is being run by the United States. But the pundits of the Walter Lippmann school are telling us that actually, due to our treaty commitments, the war is being run and must be run by SEATO, the Southeast Asia Treaty Organization. And when we read still further we learn that since SEATO is, in effect, a child of the United Nations family, the ultimate management of this war is in United Nations hands. Which means that— exactly as was the case in our Korean "police action"—everything we do to fight the Communists in Vietnam will in time be reported to, and will really be controlled by, the undersecretary of the United Nations for Political and Security Council affairs. And this position, by original agreement when the United Nations was founded, is *always* held by a Communist. If that is not insanity, it will certainly do until some even crazier arrangement can be contrived.

But that, Ladies and Gentlemen, is only the beginning of the lunacy now prevailing over Vietnam. For the next inescapable question is, when are we going to win this war—and why not? Is it possible, after our spending forty to fifty billion dollars per year on our military forces, since the memory of man runneth hardly to the contrary, that we cannot lick a puny bunch of half-starved guerillas in a country about the size of Missouri? And if we can't, why not let Chiang Kai-shek do it for us, or at least help us? He has over half a million veteran and well-trained soldiers, whose whole ambition in life is to have a chance and be allowed to fight Communists on the mainland of Asia.

In the Korean mess our government was begging other nations all over the earth to send troops to help us. We made a big fuss over the fact that Turkey sent five thousand men. But even after the Korean conflict was made a "whole new war" by Red Chinese forces, we refused—or, more accurately, the United Nations refused—to let Chiang Kai-shek participate at all. And this was despite the fact that for *this particular kind* of war his forces were worth more than those of all other potential allies put together. Are we to repeat that idiocy now? Are we to repeat it even as this "police action" gradually "escalates" into a much larger affair, with the Red Chinese involved in accordance with the obvious wishes and intentions of the administration? Who else ever refused the services, in any struggle, of a well-equipped, unusually friendly, and extremely dedicated ally who is practically right on the scene? Are we willing to allow tens of thousands and perhaps presently hundreds of thousands of American boys to be killed or crippled or captured annually for years to come instead of going ahead and fighting this war to win it with the weapons and the allies we have available?

Are the American people, having experienced all of these same combinations of treason, cross purposes, and stupidity in the Korean War, actually going to put up with them a second time? If so, some new phrase is needed for our description. Insanity is too mild a word.

This childish gullibility is made even more pathetic by the ease with which the Communists play upon it. For they know that the American people as a whole are earnestly anti-Communist, and will make more sacrifices and put up with more abuses from their own government, for the sake of fighting Communism, than for any other purpose. So the problem of how thus to get and keep the United States involved in Vietnam had, for the Communists, a very simple solution. All they needed was merely to have a few thousand of their agents and dupes and stooges stage some parades and establish some picket lines, *protesting* our being in Vietnam, and demanding that we withdraw! And at once, with the help of high ranking propagandists who are *not* recognized as pro-Communist, the American people become convinced that the Communists do not want us fighting in Vietnam; and that therefore we *must* support the administration in doing so. This ruse of getting what they want by the principle of reversal applied in this manner is so old and so familiar to the Communists that they did not even have to give it a second thought.

Yet the whole official line as to what we are doing in Vietnam is as nutty as a pecan pie, as *anybody* can see who will stop and think about it honestly for even five minutes. If our government really wanted to rout the Communists out of any area, why go ten thousand miles away to do so under such ridiculous handicaps and confusion? What's the matter with putting the same effort into an honest attempt to drive the Communists out of Cuba, right here on our doorstep, and where this Communist base is infinitely more dangerous to ourselves? This same administration has just recently gone so far in helping the Communists to reestablish their rulership in the Dominican Republic as to have military agents of our government literally and physically kidnap at gunpoint the leading anti-Communist—General Wesin y Wessin—in that country. How can anybody believe that the *same* administration is seriously interested in saving Vietnam from identically the same international Communist tyranny? The gaudy shell of pretense by which the Comsymps have promoted us into this growing war in Vietnam is so transparent and so flimsy that it would collapse under even a modicum of common sense. But how are we to get that common sense applied? Or will the American people simply never learn from experience?

Finally, we come to the sixty-four dollar question about Vietnam. What are we fighting for? What are we trying to accomplish? What are our goals? *What is our real purpose?* Nobody knows. Or, at least, nobody in the administration is willing to say. And it is only when that question is answered honestly that the whole business makes sense—and thus, paradoxically, becomes crazier than ever. For the purpose of our being at war in Vietnam, Ladies and Gentlemen, is simply: To be at war!

The ages-old advice to rulers was phrased by Shakespeare as follows: "Be it thy course to busy giddy minds with foreign quarrels." That formula is being used on the American people today with double-barreled effectiveness. For the objective is not simply to distract the attention of gullible minds from the steady advance of state socialism and government regimentation at home—although this it certainly does. But the more sinister though parallel purpose is to use the very fact of our being at war as an excuse and a means of speeding up that advance; of gradually completing the transition into state socialism, and of converting the increasing and tightening regimentation into the framework of a totalitarian police state.

Unless sufficient understanding of what is happening can be created to force a postponement of administration plans, the rationing of food and fuels, the allocation of materials, the imposition of price and wage controls, and far more drastic regulation by a central government of every detail of our daily lives are all just around a few corners not very far ahead. And the fact that we are at war is to be the excuse and the means for suppressing all opposition to such policies for brutally tightening the arbitrary enforcement of government regulations, for making all opposition to governmental policies synonymous with treason, for ruthlessly liquidating all resistance, and for irresistibly fastening the shackles of the police state around the bodies and over the lives of all the American people. To allow this to be done at all requires an ignorance of the history of the past fifty years, and a giddiness of mind with regard to what really matters, which have both been carefully induced by decades of Communist planning and propaganda. But to allow it because of our deliberate involvement in a repetition of the Korean travesty would make the occupants of any self-respecting insane asylum ashamed to have us around.

All of this process is to be helped immensely and vitally, of course, by other manifestations of lunacy to which we have been gradually and insidiously conditioned—some of which we shall be discussing further along in this very speech. It is also to be a part of a *worldwide* process going on simultaneously everywhere —with the unceasing help of our government—to bring the remaining free peoples of our planet under the same Communist one-world tyranny as ourselves. All over the earth, Ladies and Gentlemen, we see one nation after another being taken over by agents of the Kremlin who are known by everybody to be murderers, liars, and moral savages of the most depraved variety. And the top officials of our government not only treat all of these depraved beasts as human beings, and honor them and negotiate with them and build up their prestige by giving them red carpet treatment as heads of state in Washington; but agencies of our government continuously aid them in every way possible to establish and consolidate their brutal rule over the helpless people they enslave. These actions on our part amount to nothing less than insanity.

III

Or, let's look closer home. But even with regard to our domestic absurdities, let's focus briefly at first on the city of Washington.

Our government, running out of gold with which to support its own currency, and thus facing or even inviting the chaos and misery of wild inflation for our own people, continues to pour billions of American dollars in so-called foreign aid into the hands of Communist-controlled regimes abroad—which billions of dollars these regimes can convert into more gold from us on demand. This amounts to insanity. Our government, in the midst of a fight to the death with Communist enemies determined to enslave us, fills most of its high offices with men whose past records prove them to be the most favorably inclined towards Communism that can be found for the jobs. This borders on insanity, and the border is pretty thin.

One of the leading idols or heroes of the Communists in the United States, as made emphatically clear by their own pronouncements and actions, is Chief Justice Earl Warren. Yet this man, on the insistence of the Communist newspaper the *Worker*, was made chairman of an official commission to investigate the murder of a president of the United States by a known Communist. We say that this is so absurd as to approach insanity.

While we are engaged in this life-and-death struggle with Communism, our government gives the valuable boon of tax deductibility on contributions to every little left-wing, one-horse outfit which promotes Communist propaganda and purposes, and also to huge so-called foundations that are helping the Communist advance. Yet the same government refuses this same status to organizations actually opposing Communism, and is even taking it away from those that already have it. We contend that this is insane.

Our government's enforcement of even the extremely liberal and studiously prepared McCarran-Walter Immigration Law had for years been so lax and so dishonest that, on the authority of Congressman Walter himself, while he was still chairman of the House Committee on Un-American Activities, there were already more aliens illegally in this country than we had men in our total armed forces. Then the present administration put all of its prestige and pressures into emasculating and eliminating immigration restrictions almost entirely; and into thus allowing unmeasured floods of Communist-controlled aliens to enter our nation for the very purpose of helping to subjugate it to Communism. And finally we have the deal with Castro whereby *anybody* can come in from Cuba with no questions asked, which means of course that any Communist from anywhere in the world can enter our country freely and openly by merely coming *through* Cuba in the transparent guise of being a Cuban refugee.

What's more, we have been sending our planes to bring these people into Florida from Cuba, and the very first such refugee who stepped ashore from the first plane was not a Cuban at all, but a European who had previously been deported from our country as an undesirable alien. You can easily imagine the part that the Communists among these refugees will play in stirring up racial troubles in the South, and in directing these troubles to the service of Communist purposes. Actually our country is now loaded with alien Communists at key trouble-making spots everywhere, ready to create serious disorders of every kind. And we say that the whole policy our government has followed and is following with regard to immigration is dangerously insane.

Our government not only allows thousands of tons of Communist propaganda in the form of magazines and pamphlets from Soviet Russia itself and from the satellite nations to flood our country every year—and note that I said, and meant, thousands of tons—but it actually uses the facilities of the United States Post Office Department to distribute much of this Communist propaganda to individuals all over our country at what amounts to no cost at all to the Soviets. One of the many purposes served by this mail is to let good American citizens who still have relatives living in Russia or the satellite nations know that their names and American addresses are on record in Moscow or Warsaw or Prague or wherever a particular Communist magazine originates. This subtle blackmail is a tremendous deterrent to any anti-Communist action by even the most patriotic and determined anti-Commuists among these first and second generation Americans. And we content that for our government to be an active party to this gigantic blackmail scheme amounts to insanity.

But let's come now to a far more serious exhibition of lunacy. Ever since 1928 the Communists have been working steadily on the application to our country of one of the most cruel but most important formulas in their whole book of strategy. This calls for creating an ostensible revolutionary movement and demand for independence among so-called colonial peoples. Since these movements have been based on supposititious feelings and aspirations which did not really exist among the native populations, the Communist formula has called for the use of infinite cruelty and terror to force enough of such native populations to support, or to appear to support, these insurrectionary movements as to give the guerilla-made murders and vandalism some semblance of a civil war. For this minimum of fire has been needed under all of the tremendous billows of smoke in order to enable the Communists to do the rest. With the constant help of our government and the United Nations, and through propaganda, diplomatic maneuvers, and brazen audacity, the Communists have finally arranged, with regard to one colonial area after another, for those ultimate negotiations that sell out each area into a condition of theoretical independence. And this so-called independence of course, is simply a transitional stage for the new country on its way to becoming a Soviet colony or satellite.

We believe that in support of this cruel worldwide program extending over the past forty years, more human beings have been murdered, usually in the most cruel ways or by the most

horrible tortures, than at any other time or for any other purpose
in all human history. For it took this kind and quantity of
terrorization to enable Mao Tse-tung of China and Ho chi Minh
of Vietnam and Achmed Sukarno of Indonesia and Ahmed Ben
Bella of Algeria and Jomo Kenyatta of Kenya, and a dozen
others like them, even to be able to pretend that they had any
native backing in their so-called drives for freedom and independence. And always it was the best citizens among the native
populations who were tortured and murdered, while the scum
and the criminals rose towards the top in support of the Communist movement.

Now we have identically the same procedure under way with
regard to the Negroes of the United States—and simultaneously,
it just so happens, with regard to the French-speaking Catholic
population of Canada in a Communist-managed separatist movement up there. But let's stick to our own country. In 1928 the
strategy for the comrades in the United States with regard to
the Negro question was laid down in a printed pamphlet by one
John Pepper on the direct orders of Stalin. John Pepper of
course, as many of you know, was one of the many aliases of a
brilliant degenerate who, as Joseph Pogany, had been a top associate of Bela Kun throughout all the horror of the short-lived
Bela Kun Communist regime in Hungary. But it was not expected that one percent of our American Negro citizens, or
white citizens either, would ever learn who the man called John
Pepper really was—or recognize its significance if they did.

In this 1928 booklet, *American Negro Problems* (which, incidentally, we reprinted a couple of years ago by photo-offset,
and which is readily available at ten copies for one dollar from
American Opinion, Belmont, Massachusetts)—in this booklet
Pogany-Pepper established the official line that the Negroes in
the United States constituted an oppressed colony that should
be stirred to a demand for its freedom and independence, with
a separate Negro Soviet Republic to be formed out of our Dixie
states as the ultimate goal. This same theme was repeated and
further expounded in a new booklet by the Communists Ford

and Allen in 1934. Despite occasional soft-pedalling of this program, or even official backing away from this theme, for tactical reasons, the same basis of Communist agitation and goal of Communist activity has been maintained and made increasingly clear to all American Communists, white and black, right up to the present time. And as recently as June of 1964, the executive committee of the Communist Party, U.S.A., made a quiet new distribution of thousands of copies of the Ford and Allen 1934 booklet—which was entitled *The Negroes in a Soviet America*. And incidentally, again simply for documentation, exact reprints of that booklet are also available from American Opinion at three copies for one dollar.

Now the point of all of this is that what has been happening in the South, and even in Harlem and Los Angeles and other places, including the increasing racial turmoil of the past several years, does not make sense unless you realize what the Communists behind all of this agitation are trying to accomplish. Nor will the spreading riots and murders and vandalism of the future make sense unless you understand the Communist plans to terrorize the ordinary loyal Negro American citizens into supporting, or appearing to support, this drive for a separate, independent Negro Soviet Republic to be carved right out of the United States.

In carrying out this scheme, and to support propaganda based on it, not only will thousands of white citizens in the South be murdered by the comparatively few Negro criminals who can be inflamed by the Communists to the point of actually participating in the terror, but—exactly as for the Moslems in Algeria —tens of thousands of the best Negro citizens themselves will be tortured and killed as a part of the terrorization necessary to establish some Communist Negro leader at the head of what will be called a Negro Revolutionary Movement for freedom and independence.

And the Negroes themselves will be by far the heaviest sufferers from this brutal tyranny. The first brazen warning to the Negroes of the terror to be inflicted on them unless they fall in line has already appeared in the Perry Smaw case. Here was an eighty-nine year old Negro farmer and landowner in Greensboro, Alabama, who was quite proud of the country that had enabled him to live a happy and successful life; who appreciated the true friendship and respect of his white neighbors, which he had enjoyed all of that life; who could see the Communist plans and hands at work in the trouble and rioting and bitterness being created under the slogan of "civil rights"; and who was trying bravely and determinedly, in his small but effective way, to warn his fellow Negroes of the folly of letting themselves be used by the Communists. In fact he was going downtown to speak on the subject several nights per week to all that he could get to listen. And so, this good, wise, and truly patriotic American Negro, eighty-nine years old, was beaten so badly with an iron skillet that he died without ever regaining consciousness. But note that his tongue was cut out before he was killed so as to make the warning to other Negroes emphatically clear. This was typical of the kind of cruelties which the FLN Communists had perpetrated on their fellow Moslems in Algeria, on an average of twenty such atrocities per day for seven years, for identically the same purpose of intimidation. And it is exactly what we have said for years would be happening in the South as soon as the Communists behind the "civil rights" fraud were ready to go that far on their plotted course.

Now all of this is absolutely clear to anybody who will take the trouble to read the Communists' own publications and directions on the subject, with any background knowledge of how they have now used exactly the same formula in so many other countries. All of this is bound to be known by many people in high positions in our federal government. Yet by far the greatest help the Communists have had in advancing this program—help without which they could not even have established the foundations for their progress—and the most powerful support of those very agitators who are following this Communist blueprint for the eventual dismemberment of our country have come from the actions of our federal government or of various officials in that government. And we contend that these actions border on insanity.

In fact, as we review the whole picture, far more extensive and panoramic than I have been able to paint it here, of all that Washington is doing to aid Communist purposes in this country —not just in connection with the Negro Revolutionary Movement, but in so many other ways—we cannot help remembering the old Spanish adage that in the land of the blind the one-eyed is king. Acting on that principle and assuming that it applies to mental as well as physical sight, we are considering a campaign to gather and send to Washington a trainload of half-wits. This ought to assure a considerable improvement without making the change so rapid and so complete as to disturb the apathetic somnolence of the American people.

IV

But now let's leave Washington busily braiding the rope with which to hang itself, and look around us everywhere. Unfortunately the story is very much the same whether it is from the world of education, or the press, or religion, or entertainment that we select our items for comment. As we shall indicate by simply mixing them up a bit.

Today a grade school teacher is not allowed to have the children say a prayer or read Bible verses in her classroom, while letting them shoot dice or stamp on the American flag is considered permissible, and in some high educational circles even praiseworthy. We contend that this borders on insanity.

Today many good Christians continue to contribute to their churches, knowing full well that some of their money thus goes to the National Council of Churches, while high-ranking committees of the National Council of Churches put out reading lists recommending some of the most blasphemous books ever published in America, and pornographic books with passages so vile that these passages cannot even be sent through the mails in letters of complaint. We say that this approaches insanity.

In 1960 the man who is now president of the United States was running simultaneously for two offices; on the national ticket for the vice-presidency, and in Texas for reelection to his seat in the United States Senate. And on issue after issue, the platforms of these two campaigns were diametrically opposed to each other. In other words, here was a candidate for very high offices—one of which could lead and did lead directly to the presidency—who was brazenly and *officially* talking out of both sides of his mouth throughout the whole campaign. And we contend that the American press could have ignored this incredible hypocrisy so nearly unanimously, and the American people could have swallowed it so readily, only in a world which has practically gone crazy.

On Monday, January 11, 1965, the invited speaker at a *compulsory* school assembly of Mount Mercy College, a private Catholic school for girls in Pittsburgh, Pennsylvania, was Bayard Rustin. The school has some seven hundred students. Mr. Rustin, it will be remembered, was chief organizer of the so-called march on Washington in August 1963—which march fitted so well into Communist designs for trouble-making and propaganda.

Mr. Rustin also has in his record a string of jail sentences and arrests for various offences. These include at least one arrest and conviction involving sexual perversion. He once served as organizer for the Young Communist League, and boasts of affiliation with many organizations which have been officially cited as Communist fronts by various government agencies. And more recently he distinguished himself by expressing his resentment over the rescue from sadistic Communist-inspired Congo savages of some of the Europeans and Americans these savages were murdering, including Catholic priests and nuns. And we contend that for the Catholic heads of this girls' college to invite this man to be an official speaker at a compulsory assembly is sheer insanity.

John Birch was an American boy who went directly from theological school to become a missionary in China. When we got into the war against Japan, John volunteered for service, joined General Chennault's 14th United States Air Force in Chungking, and during the next three years, through a combination of brilliance and bravery, became almost a legend while he was still alive. Ten days after the war was over John Birch, as a captain in the United States Army, in uniform but on a peaceful mission, was brutally killed by Chinese Communists near Hsuchow, China—apparently to prevent the leadership, knowledge, and inspiration which they knew he would provide in opposition to Communism in China.

Since I wrote my small biography of John Birch in 1954 I have met or heard from many men who knew him during his years of service in China. Their comment, to a man, can be summed up in the words of another associate whom I quoted in my book. It was: "I came as near to worshipping John Birch as any man I have ever known." His nobility of character and of purpose was unsurpassed, and he was beyond all question one of the finest young men and greatest heroes America has ever produced. Yet, Ladies and Gentlemen, during the past two years there has been started, and pushed forward on several college campuses, a purely paper organization known as the Tao Chu Kwang Society. Nobody knows the name of the Chinese Communist who bayonetted the unarmed John Birch to death. And of course his name could have been Tao Chu Kwang. So the small advertisements of this fictitious society say: "Let's call him Tao Chu Kwang, and use that name for our group." In short, these American college youngsters have now been so brainwashed in favor of Communism that they promote an organization for the specific purpose of honoring the Communist murderer of John Birch. And this, we contend, is typical of the insanity now creeping over America.

Lenin once told his followers: "We must hate—hatred is the basis of Communism. Children must be taught to hate their parents if the parents are not Communists." And Anatole Lunacharski, former Soviet commissar of education, once said: "Down with love of one's neighbors. What we need is hatred.

We must know how to hate; only thus shall we conquer the universe."

Now one of our great cardinal principles in The John Birch Society is that we do not hate anybody. We do not even hate Earl Warren; we hate only the evil principles and purposes which we think he represents. We do not hate any evil men, but only the evil which they do, and evil itself as an abstract force in a world which we hope to make better. Yet the Communists, following their formula of always accusing their enemies of exactly what they themselves are doing, and of always exactly reversing all truth and even all language, refer to The John Birch Society unceasingly as a *hate group*, and succeed in having us so labeled, automatically, in that sizable percentage of the American press which, unwittingly or not, slavishly follows the Communist line. So the American people come to accept the charge that we—and not the Communists—are indulging in and fomenting hatred as a part of contemporary existence. And we contend that this acceptance by the public of so blatant a reversal of the truth, in this as in a thousand other manifestations by the Communists of the formula of exact reversal at work—that this childish folly is so great as to border on insanity.

On New Year's Day, 1965, a group of several Protestant ministers, representing four denominations—and including Canon Robert Cromey, a special assistant to Episcopal Bishop James A. Pike—gave a ball in California Hall, San Francisco, for known homosexuals in the area. Much to the disgust and concern of the local police, there were some six hundred homosexuals and their friends present at the party—for which a dance permit had been issued. Police Chief Thomas Cahill stated that his men had been required to police the affair after they understood that tickets were being sold at the door and liquor was being sold inside. And because these police found it necessary to make five or six arrests—most of which seemed to have been deliberately provoked—the San Francisco *Chronicle* carried a story on Sunday, January 3, with the headline "Incidents at a Homosexual Benefit," and then a larger headline: "Angry Ministers Rip Police."

In other words, the real complaint was against the police for interfering in any way with the boys having their fun at this public party given them by clergymen. And this whole affair, we contend, is a frightening measure and example of the atmosphere of insanity which is now permeating our daily lives.

V

And so, my fellow inmates! Let me remind you of the woman who sued her husband for divorce on the grounds that he was continuously drunk. "How long have you been married?" asked the judge. "Three years, Your Honor," she replied. "And how long has this continual drunkenness been going on?" persisted the judge. "Ever since I first met him, Your Honor, six months before we were married." "Then why on earth," the judge now asked, "have you waited this long to complain about this condition?" "Because, Your Honor," the lady replied ruefully, "it was not until last Wednesday, which was the first time I ever saw him sober, that I *realized* he had been drunk ever since I had known him!"

My point is that if you do not think you are living in what amounts to a gigantic insane asylum today, it is because you have become so accustomed to the manifestations of insanity all around you that you do not even recognize the condition. And it is the function and duty of The John Birch Society to bring a sound sense of values and some basic sanity back onto the scene; and to have more and more people stop and think just what idiocy they are accepting as a normal part of life.

But when you start meditating about this madness all around us, you are soon struck by the fact that there is too much method in it. It is not insanity on the part of the conspirators, who are thus conditioning the American people for destruction, but only on the part of their victims. For every item falls in place on one of just two roads. These are the roads of collectivism and of immorality, which come together eventually into the slave compound known as Communism. For the Communists to impose their tyranny on America and maintain it, they must have the people gradually come to take for granted that there can be no questioning of either a central government's power or its wisdom. Even the most idiotic and unjustifiable extension of the fingers of government into our daily lives and actions must come to seem commonplace. And similarly, all conscience and all morality must be gradually eroded away, until an individual's responsibility for his own immoral actions is completely forgotten in a flood of conformity to amoral customs on every side. Finally, the individual becomes resigned to a generally accepted doctrine that he has no rights or privileges or possessions except those which the state confers upon him. Finally, also, the individual's soul and conscience are crushed by an all-pervading moral nihilism into a hopeless confusion and despair. Then and only then can the Communists rule *"peacefully,"* as they would put it, meaning with all resistance or even potential resistance effectively destroyed. And they can then do so in accordance with standardized Communist practice, by brute force and terror, with no real concern about any other motivation on the part of their subjects than hunger and fear.

The truth is, Ladies and Gentlemen, that for more than forty years this incredibly diabolic conspiracy of criminals, seeking ever more power and glory and perquisites for its members, has been engaged in a subtle but gigantic program to destroy the three great basic human loyalties: Loyalty to God, loyalty to country, and loyalty to family. They aim at—in fact, from their point of view, they simply must have—a social organization in which there is no other loyalty possible except to themselves, or to the state which represents the structure of their power.

The constant advances all around us today of collectivism and immorality have not just happened; and have not even been due directly to the weaknesses of human nature, except as these weaknesses have been insidiously but aggressively played upon by agents of a conspiratorial nerve center which knew exactly what it was doing. And little by little in degree, while larger and larger in extensiveness, these planned and fomented movements down the paths of collectivism and immorality have now reached so far, that we are living in a complete bedlam of political, economic, spiritual, and moral confusion which approaches insanity.

Let us remind you of Pavlov's dogs, and of the seriousness with which the Communists have treated those experiments. The trainer takes a healthy and intelligent dog and teaches him first to follow and obey a series of varied signals in order to obtain food and kind treatment. Then suddenly the whole series is changed, the old signals or the dog's reactions to them no longer work, and the confused animal must somehow learn to interpret and follow the new directions. Or, translating this into the human terms in which the Communists are really interested, the dog has had to accept a new sense of values. Then by the time this is barely accomplished, the signals are all changed again. The dog has to forget the second set, as well as traces of the first one; and, striving desperately to do what is expected of him, spurred on by both his need for food and his need for kindness, he somehow gradually grasps and follows enough of the new combination of directions and reactions to give him *some* food and more hope.

But next, even this third set of signals and compliances fails to bring the expected results. All has been changed again. This time, to make the confusion, frustration, and despair even greater, various signals out of each of the three earlier sets are now combined in the series, so that the poor dog is hopelessly bewildered. This process continues, of changing the signals, of putting in entirely new ones, altering the meaning of earlier ones, reversing the significance of those that have been learned, and otherwise making both memory and experience appear useless as guides to action. It goes on until the dog, still trying frantically and pitifully to understand and comply with what is wanted of him, accepting as right what all his past experience tells him is wrong, struggling to his utmost to fit into this insane environment in which he is a captive—or again, in human terms, having lost *all* sense of values—the poor dog at last breaks down mentally, and becomes a whining idiot. After this stage is reached, he can once again be taught to perform the very simplest and most monotonous acts over and over for the sake of his daily food, but all intelligence, all spirit, and all hope have disappeared and left but a vacant stare.

And let me urge you, Ladies and Gentlemen, as solemnly as I possibly can, to feel great pity for the dog of our illustration and to take heed from his fate. You had better have sympathy for the dog, for exactly the same thing is happening to yourselves. You have already been brought to the stage where you are losing all memory of what is right and wrong, discarding all experience, and denying that any sound and permanent sense of values even exists. The conspirators have only a few steps further to go and the desperately bewildered American citizen, like Pavlov's dogs, will be ready to believe anything he is told, do anything he is ordered, and gratefully accept anything he is given by his master, the Communist state.

Your clergymen's party for the homosexuals; the sending of American boys to die in Korea—or in Vietnam—where both sides of a sham and play-acting war are directed by the same influences; the driving of families out of their homes and neighborhood roots by that gigantic and cold-blooded invitation to fraud known as urban renewal; the constant stream of falsehoods and distortions in the American press or over the air; the efforts to make criminals out of our local police and heroes out of our criminals; the filling of half the drugstores in America with blasphemous and pornographic books and magazines; the constant honoring, even by the very heads of our own government, and also by great commercial and professional organizations, and by great universities, of men who are known by everybody to be murderers, liars, traitors, and degenerates of the most vicious order; the attempted conversion of our whole educational system into a vast training ground for the destruction of every sound sense of values and of all but the most criminal ambitions; the deliberate fomenting of friction and bitterness between Catholics and Protestants, between Jews and Gentiles, between whites and blacks, between management and labor; these and a thousand other manifestations of the successful progress of the Communist program now surround us on every side. And they do not have to be carried too much further now before only the Communist bosses already in the highest positions, and holding all of the reins in their hands, will be the ones to know where and how thousands of ostensibly independent or spontaneous activities fit into the colossal puzzle they have created. Only these top Communists will know who is an agent of theirs, carrying out their plans and instructions as against the vast majority of gullible dupes or opportunistic cowards being led by the nose into such activities. The confusion will be so complete, and the sense of futility on the part of even informed anti-Communists so great, that most of them will throw up their hands in despair, and decide to drift at last with what seems to be an irrevocable tide. Or at least this is the result which the Communists have intended. Breaking the will of people to resist —that is to resist anything, no matter how idiotic it ought to sound—is at the very core of Communist strategy.

VI

Well, Ladies and Gentlemen, what we have been reviewing are Communist plans and methods. But we do not have to let those plans be carried out to completion. Actually the solution to all of this is very simple. But it is by no means easy. In fact it is as huge and difficult a job as the Communists planned it should be by the time they reached this point in their advance towards absolute enslavement of the total population of the earth.

The size of the task, however, does not make it impossible. For its simplicity is all-important. We must start by preserving our sanity. And by this I mean—to use once again a phrase which I have repeated so often in this speech—by maintaining at all costs a sound, traditional, and morally based sense of values. If enough Americans would stand firmly enough on this foundation, it would be impossible for Communist deceptions, pressures, and propaganda to keep on sweeping us further down the two roads of collectivism and immorality. To that end it is up to each of us to do his part; first by making sure of his own position, and second by persuading others to do the same.

As to the immense derangement, so cunningly created all around us, there is a very simple compass by which each individual can guide himself. All that is necessary, as we have pointed out many times before, is for every civilized and patriotic man or woman to fall back on the moral code of the days when we really had one; and to judge every action of themselves and of others strictly by that moral code, without modification or exception. For in this increasing confusion of propaganda, appeasement, expediency, false leadership, and deceptive pretenses, there simply is no other criterion by which any good citizen can safely determine his course. Simply remember, firmly and confidently, that morality sees further than intellect.

But this is not enough. Let's emphasize this statement by looking first at the road to collectivism. There are many excellent lecturers and leaders throughout the country who are giving some very sound courses today on the follies and crimes of too much government and on the value and necessity of the resolution by individuals to conduct their own lives and affairs strictly according to the principles of a free enterprise economy. We are all for these teachers, because few things are needed more now than to reconvert brainwashed American business and professional men back to a belief in classical economics. And each one who is persuaded to eschew collectivism at every turn in his own economic affairs, even when it would be temporarily to his advantage, is setting an example and having an impact which are of great value to the conservative cause. But the practical chances of stopping the Communists simply by this process are today entirely negligible.

In anything approaching a normal world, having enough lecturers preach this doctrine convincingly enough to enough listeners so as eventually to turn the tide back from collectivism towards complete non-intervention by government, should be entirely possible. But when you have an enemy army marching over the hill determined to destroy your city, you do not prevent this catastrophe by telling everybody in sight simply to go on about his business as usual. The army of our Communist enemies is far worse, because these enemies wear no uniforms, do not march in visible formation, and are creeping up on our city imperceptibly but steadily from every side. And any thought that if you pay no attention to this great hostile tribe and simply act yourself in the soundest peaceful traditions, the enemy will disappear, is a dangerous fallacy. Just as is the thought that if each individual American himself becomes strictly a free enter-priser, the threat of collectivism will go away. The cold, hard fact is that the collectivist armies are now tightly managed and ruthlessly driven forward by criminal masters who are not them-selves susceptible to reason; and who are both able and deter-mined to see that such reason does not even reach their marching minions simply from a relatively few thousand converts who are setting a good example. These converts, to do their real duty today, simply must add their weight and leadership to the organ-ized forces that are striving to stop the collectivist hordes.

Second, the same thing is true with regard to the road to immorality. We do not have any chance of stopping the Com-munists from carrying our whole nation down that road at a stampeding rate simply by persuading enough individuals to say to themselves tomorrow: "Henceforth I'll do nothing which could cause even a twinge to my conscience." It is terribly im-portant, but it is not enough today, merely to be a good person yourself and to set a good example. The forces of evil are too well organized, too solidly entrenched, and too far advanced for there to be enough time left for the process of individual ex-ample and conversion to save our religious ideals, our civilization, our freedom, or our lives. It is not enough today to be a good person, but the weight and leadership of good individuals must be added to the organized and concerted action of all other good individuals if we are to save even our spiritual inheritance from such powerful and ruthless destroyers as now assail us on every side.

So my point is not, in the mood of a devout preacher or a wise teacher, merely to urge upon our members and friends that they themselves be truly good individuals, and responsibly self-reliant. Most of them already are. Otherwise they would not be either members of, or prospects for membership in, The John Birch Society. What I am trying to make clear is that we need the concerted, mutually encouraging, *organized* effort of all such people in order to stand up to, stop, and eventually rout the extremely well organized and brilliantly directed enemies who intend to enslave us. In brief, working together by example and precept and labor and leadership, let's try to start bringing some sanity back into American life, and then help it to grow until it becomes a mighty burst of common sense and traditional values, relighting the whole American scene.

Two Revolutions at Once

This article was first published in pamphlet form in April 1965.

The farmer had seen many pictures of a giraffe. But he simply refused to believe them. His insistence that the giraffe was purely a product of somebody's mischievous imagination was repeated until it became an obsession with him. Then one day while the circus was in town, a giraffe slipped his moorings and eventually wound up out in the country, hungrily grazing the top leaves of a tree in this farmer's front yard. Just as several attendants from the circus, and a number of excited neighbors, were closing in on the scene, one such neighbor dashed into the house through the back door. In urgent tones he explained what was happening. Reluctantly, the farmer came out of his front door and took a good look at the whole tableau, including the browsing giraffe only ten feet away. "Pfui," said the farmer, turning on his heels and going back into the house. "What a lot of nonsense over nothing. I still say that there ain't no such animal."

UNLIKE THE FARMER in the above fable, a preponderant majority of the American people will not even take a good look at the beast known as Communism; not even when that beast has gone on a vicious and dangerous rampage right in their own yard. When we begin these pages with two or three statements of simple and historical truth, many good people whose minds we would like to reach will immediately drop the pamphlet in the wastebasket. They have now acquired such a vested interest in the error that "there ain't no such animal," as to shy away at once from any chance of being confused by the facts.

For those who are honest enough, however, and reasonable enough, to be willing to listen, let's review very briefly the whole story now known as "civil rights." To the informed we shall offer nothing new. To the uninformed we shall simply try to repeat, summarize, and synthesize some of the known facts that are necessary for an understanding of the horror that is now upon us.

The action could plausibly be said to have begun on the Pacific coast of Asia some forty-five years ago. But the thinking and planning behind this action go much further back. The whole concept was rooted in one of the original and biggest of all the Communist Big Lies. This lie is that Communism is an uprising of the downtrodden masses against bosses who exploit them. The record is absolutely clear that precisely the opposite is true. Communism is always imposed from the top down, never achieved from the bottom up. The idea that Communism is sought by the masses, who are prevented from having it by reactionary upper classes, is one of those exact reversals of the truth which are so customary and so useful in Communist strategy.

In its now completely visible reality, Communism is simply and wholly a conspiracy of ruthless and powerful criminals in the very top social, economic, educational, and political circles of their respective countries and of the whole world. The objective of these conspirators is to increase their power and extend it downward until the international Communist hierarchy has established a rigid and absolute tyranny over the total population of our planet. The condition of the masses, as these "masters of deceit" are fully aware, will always and everywhere actually be made worse by Communist success in every country which they subjugate and add to their empire of slaves. And if you do not think that this reversal of the truth has anything to do with American "civil rights," you are badly mistaken.

For out of this basic Big Lie evolved the strategy of "anti-colonialism"—sometimes known by such other names as "national liberation" and "anti-imperialism" and "self-determination." The supposedly oppressed native populations of other continents, ruled or dominated and "exploited" by the "imperialistic" nations of Europe, were to be stirred into demands for their freedom and independence. This derivative of the Big Lie involved, in itself, two lies of immense importance. In the first place, with regard to the premise: By 1920, the French in Indochina or in Algeria, the Dutch in Indonesia, the Belgians in the Congo, and other "imperialistic" powers were giving their colonial subjects a very enlightened and benevolent rule indeed. They were gradually raising the standard of living, the level of education, the exercise of individual freedom and responsibility, and the participation of the natives in their own local governments as rapidly as these advances of civilization could be absorbed.

This process was not necessarily or primarily the result of any noble or altruistic forces at work. It was developing automatically from an enlightened self-interest; and from the commercial progress in colonial areas, which was being promoted by pioneers from the mother countries to the advantage of the native populations as well as of themselves. As a consequence of the total influences which were prevalent, the natives were coming more and more to regard themselves as actual or potential citizens of, and certainly as loyal parts and members of, those great empires of which London or Paris or Lisbon or The Hague might be the capital. There was no more spontaneous demand or natural desire for "independence" among any of these colonial peoples in 1920 than there was among the French-speaking Canadians in 1950 or the American Negroes in 1955. The whole appearance of these "separatist" movements had to be artificially created.

In the second place, with regard to the pretended objective: The "independence" to be achieved was intended to be, and in fact always became, merely a temporary transition stage between an enlightened western European "colonialism" and the infinitely brutal Soviet colonialism. Each new emerging nation, like Indonesia or Algeria, was allowed to go through the motions and to carry on the pretense of being independent, merely as a step on the way to becoming a recognized part of the Soviet *colonial empire*. And again, both the material and spiritual living conditions of these "colonial" peoples have always been made drastically worse than before the Communists began interfering in their affairs.

Just imagine, for instance, how wonderful it would seem today to the inhabitants of Ghana under Kwame Nkrumah, or to those of North Vietnam under Ho chi Minh, if they could be back under the peaceful and benign colonial rule, respectively, of England and of France.

Communism has brought horror and misery and slavery to all such people before whom it held up the lure of "freedom and independence." Yet, as already indicated, it was as early as 1920 —two years before the USSR itself was established—that the Communists were sending their agents up and down eastern Asia from Mukden to Singapore to begin agitation among the "colonial" peoples for "freedom and independence." And by 1927 the first worldwide Communist front, the League Against Imperialism, was founded in Brussels, Belgium, to promote the same theme. Among the leaders who established this Communist propaganda agency were Albert Einstein from Germany, Romain Rolland from France, J. Nehru from India, and Mohammed Hatta from Indonesia. The whole concern of the league, of course, was with the horrid imperialism practiced by the western European nations (and by the United States!!). You can be sure that this league and these men had no slightest worry about Soviet imperialism.

II. The Basic Formula

Let us reassure you once again that we really are still dealing with the immediate background to, and even important elements of, the American "civil rights" movement. As will become clear in due course. But first we need to show how this "anti-colonialism" strategy has worked in actual operation. And Algeria offers an excellent case history for that purpose.

In 1954 there were in Algeria approximately 8,000,000 native Moslems; 1,250,000 French settlers or descendants of French settlers; and 250,000 Jews—many of whom, or whose ancestors, had also come from France. (This last fact proved eventually to be of considerable value to the anti-Communist cause. For few developments have served more effectively to wake up intelligent Jews in other countries to the realities of Communism, as against the falsehoods being fed to them, than what happened to their coreligionists in Algeria.) French citizens with pioneer instincts had been moving across the Mediterranean into Algeria since 1830. They had carried with them the purposes, knowledge, and methods needed to convert this northern edge of the Sahara Desert into a great commercial and civilized part of the French empire. And they were rapidly integrating the native Moslems into every phase of this happy development.

Algeria was not even technically a colony—as were Tunisia or Guinea—but consisted legally of several additional "departments" of France itself. The Moslem natives had come to regard themselves as "French," and were increasingly proud of being a part of the French nation. And as late as 1954 there were not five percent of the total population of Algeria who had the slightest interest in forming an "independent" country of their own—any more than there are five percent of the American Negroes with any such interest today.

But the time had come when it fitted into overall Communist plans to apply the anti-colonialism strategy to this area. So a murderous guerilla band was formed under a Communist criminal named Ben Bella, and was given the high-sounding title of the Federation for National Liberation—or FLN. Then the standard formula which lies at the center of this Communist strategy was put to work. Enough natives had to be persuaded by propaganda, or terrorized by atrocities, or impelled by the combination into supporting this "national liberation" movement, or into appearing to do so, to give some semblance of a "civil war." And the FLN campaign for that purpose developed into guerilla activities averaging some twenty atrocities per day for the next seven years.

Of course the French government, under fully as much Communist influence as ours is under now, was in many ways a clandestine partner to the actions and purposes of the FLN. So the people of France were told, by *government and press*, about atrocities being perpetrated by the FLN in Algeria *on the French settlers there and on French army personnel*. These would seem to be the actions of a revolutionary people almost fanatically fighting for their independence. Neither the French people, nor the American people and the rest of the world, were allowed to learn that practically the total effort of the FLN guerillas was spent in afflicting atrocities on their fellow Moslems, who wanted no part of any such revolution. For this would have given the show away.

In time, these pro-Communist forces in France made their one big mistake of sending Jacques Soustelle to Algeria as governor general. Because of his extremely liberal and pro-de Gaulle background, it was assumed that Soustelle would be entirely sympathetic to the FLN. As he clearly was, when he first took up his new duties. His attitude seems to have been about as follows: Well, it is certainly too bad that these revolutionary troops are killing French army officers. But after all, they are seeking the independence of their country, and the French army is the force preventing that independence. So what can you expect? And it is too bad that these revolutionary troops should be killing some French settlers. But these settlers undoubtedly have a feudal attitude that stands in the way of independence, so who can blame the FLN? You cannot make an omelet without breaking eggs, nor achieve the independence of a nation without shedding blood.

But Jacques Soustelle happened to be intellectually honest.

And in the course of a very few months he discovered to his amazement certain incontrovertible truths about the whole situation that had been unknown to him and to most of the people in France. These included the following:

(1) There *was* no revolutionary force in Algeria that amounted to anything in a military sense. The FLN could be completely wiped out by the French army there at any time the army was instructed or even allowed to do so. In fact, the FLN *was* practically wiped out on several occasions, but was promptly restored as a guerilla force through reinforcements kept in Morocco or Tunisia for that purpose.

(2) The atrocities which the FLN were able to inflict on French army personnel were relatively few and far between. They consisted primarily of the occasional capture of some detached individual officer, who would then be deliberately crippled and maimed and carted around the countryside in a slatted cage too small for his body. This was to show the natives the supposed contempt of the FLN for the French army, and what might happen to anybody who opposed the FLN.

(3) The atrocities which the FLN perpetrated on the French settlers were also comparatively few, because the FLN did not have the force to get at these victims through the protection provided by the French army and the loyal natives. The FLN was primarily capable of sudden hit-and-run attacks on isolated native villages.

(4) The numerous and cruel atrocities of the FLN "revolutionaries," which constituted almost their whole occupation, were inflicted on their fellow native Moslems—for the purpose we have indicated above.

(5) There was no real sentiment for revolution, nor for independence, nor for separation from France, among the native population at all—except as the Communists were able to coerce and simulate such sentiment through their threats, pressures, and cruelties.

(6) The opposition to the FLN and loyalty to France amid

the native Moslems wherever they had the opportunity to show that loyalty or the strength to stand in opposition—as among the thirty thousand tightly knit followers of one famous Moslem leader, the Bachaga Boualam—were overwhelming.

(7) But the pretense that this was honestly a civil war for "freedom and independence"; the maintenance of a "provisional revolutionary government" of Algeria under Nasser's wing in Cairo; these and all other parts of the great deception were being maintained in order to support the propaganda and diplomatic pressures throughout the world—and especially in and through the United Nations—for Algerian "independence." This independence—meaning the turning of Algeria over to the Communist rule of the FLN regime under Ben Bella—was to be won, as it eventually was won, by *negotiations*. And these negotiations were to be made plausible, or at least possible, through these spurious claims given substance only by terror.

As a result of these discoveries and revelations, Soustelle soon became the most determined and powerful fighter for keeping Algeria French, and against the Communist capture of this "colony." But it was too late, and the total forces against him were too strong. Members of the international Communist conspiracy in the United Nations, in Moscow, in the French government, and in our government, all working in smooth concert and each one knowing exactly what he was doing—while confusing everybody else by deception within deception and pretense on top of pretense—had all resistance too completely stymied and under control.

Eventually tens of thousands of the finest officers and men in the French army, seeing themselves being deliberately betrayed by de Gaulle, took the desperate step of forming the OAS (Secret Army Organization) to try to save Algeria from Communist hands. But their leader, General Salan, was too patriotic to carry this struggle to Metropolitan France itself. De Gaulle used that major part of the French army which, however reluctantly and bitterly, still followed the "route of discipline," to help the

FLN to destroy the OAS. Just as the administration in Washington is visibly planning to use the U. S. army, to whatever extent necessary, to suppress opposition to the leaders of the Negro Revolutionary Movement in the South. And de Gaulle and his fellow Communists finally carried out their aim, at Evian, of *negotiating* all of Algeria into the Communist hands of Ben Bella's FLN, as a supposedly "free and independent" nation.

Then began those continuous tortures and cruel massacres of tens of thousands of the Harkis. These were the native Algerian Moslems, including members of the local police forces, who had been most faithful to France—of which terror, incidentally, you have read practically nothing in your American press. This is simply a preview of what the NRM—the Negro Revolutionary Movement—will do to the people of the South, both white and black but especially the blacks, who oppose their treasonous movement, if and when they succeed in setting up their "free and independent" Negro Soviet Republic out of our southern states.

Also to be noted as of great importance in the parallel which we are attempting to foreshadow is another Communist accomplishment. The various steps and developments over several years by which this complete betrayal of a part of France was ultimately accomplished were such that the final result served as a terrific demoralization to the anti-Communist leadership, and boost to the Communist forces, in Metropolitan France itself. The specific "revolution" in Algeria was made to serve as a vital part of the broader "proletarian" revolution being conducted by the French Communists at home. The anti-colonialism *racket*, in and with regard to Algeria, had not only made a Communist colony out of this former French "colony," but had tremendously undermined the mother country as well. And this should be kept vividly in mind in connection with the *two simultaneous revolutions* which the Communists actually boast that they are now carrying on within the United States.

III. The Agitation for a Negro Soviet Republic

Now, with this highly condensed introduction, we must come to the application of identically the same Communist formula to a part of the United States—as Algeria was a part of France. Remember that the Communists always use every possible difference in language, color, race, or religion out of which to create bitterness, turmoil, civil disorders, and as much semblance of civil war as they can. In Algeria they had a slight color difference, a stronger racial difference, and a complete religious difference on which to build their evil machinations. In the United States they have a complete color and racial difference; and at times have probably been behind the attempt through the Black Muslim movement to bring a religious difference into play if they can.

There are many other correspondences in the two situations. And without grasping the parallel, or the more important fact that a general formula, utilized by the Communists over and over in other parts of the world with only such adaptations as local circumstances make necessary, has been applied to an area of France and is now being applied to an area of the United States—without understanding this background there is no chance of understanding what is really taking place in our southern states today.

The League Against Imperialism, you will recall, was put together by the Communists in 1927. And by the next year the Soviets were ready to make clear to the comrades in America that exactly the same theme of "anti-colonialism" was to be applied in this country with respect to the Negro population in the southeastern quarter. The Negroes were to be regarded as an oppressed and exploited *colony* which should be stirred and agitated—and eventually terrorized—into an appearance of seeking its "freedom and independence."

The official line was laid down in the booklet *American Negro Problems* by John Pepper, published in 1928. Pepper was one of the many aliases used by Moscow's agent Joseph Pogany, who had been one of the top men in the incredibly cruel but short-lived Bela Kun Communist regime in Hungary. He was now sent by Stalin to the United States specifically to lay the groundwork for the agitation which would eventually develop into a Negro Revolutionary Movement in America. In his booklet you will find such passages as the following:

The Workers (Communist) Party of America, in its fight against imperialism, must recognize clearly the tremendous revolutionary possibilities of the liberation movement of the Negro people.

The word Communist, in parentheses, to identify clearly the Workers party, appears as above in the original. Also, note the key words "against imperialism," and "liberation," of the worldwide Communist program and propaganda.

The "black belt" of the south . . . *constitutes virtually a colony within the body of the United States of America.*

The italics are in the original, because this sentence sets forth the core of the Communist strategy.

The Communist Party of America must recognize the right of national self-determination for the Negroes and must respect their own decision about the form of the realization of this self-determination. The *Negro* Communists should emphasize in their propaganda *the establishment of a Negro Soviet Republic*.

Here, handed down in permanent form by one of the most vicious Communist murderers Moscow has ever employed (but also one of the most brilliant), was the directive for the long-range program in our country which is still being carried out today. And despite a certain hedging by the Communists at present about their ultimate aims—exactly as Mao Tse-tung and Sukarno and Castro hedged for a considerable period at one time in their careers about being Soviet agents—the final terroristic stage of that program is right now getting under way in what the Communists call the "black belt states."

The hedging became strategically advisable for a number of reasons. One was that as a whole the Negroes in America, even in the South, have so much higher living standards and are much more literate than were the "oppressed natives" in any other so-called "colony" anywhere else in the world. So that the means of communication among them, and between them and the remainder of their country, were so much greater and more pervasive than had been the case for the natives of Indonesia or the savages of Ghana.

Another reason was that the percentage of their supposed "oppressors"—namely, the white people of the South—was so much larger than had been, for instance, the percentage of Frenchmen in Algeria to the Moslem population. And still another was that there were millions of Negroes in Harlem and Chicago and other northern cities whom the Communists wanted to agitate, and embitter over supposed grievances, and utilize in their general plans for subversion of the country as a whole. Because of these and various other circumstances, the idea of converting the Dixie states into a Negro Soviet Republic was harder to promote, and had more embarrassing ramifications and disadvantages, than did the fraudulent theme of "self-determination" for the Moslems in Algeria or the "colonial" peoples anywhere else.

So this hedging was begun, and this problem for the Communists of what they at first called "the two aspects of the revolution which is developing in this country," was given an official solution in another booklet, published in 1934. It bore the very carefully chosen title of *The Negroes in a Soviet America*, and was written by the Communists James W. Ford and James S. Allen. The latter part of the booklet discusses "The Combination of Two Revolutions," and contains such passages as the following.

The revolution for land and freedom in the South and the proletarian revolution in the country as a whole will develop hand in hand. Each will lend strength and support to the other. The working class— both white and Negro—will lead both.

Here a touch of the old Communist formula of "agrarian reform" is being added to the brew.

Revolution is not a matter of our own choosing. It is forced upon us by capitalism itself, which degrades us, grinds us down into the dust, makes life unbearable.

The twenty million Negroes in America undoubtely own more automobiles, more bathtubs, and more television sets—and more freedom and more opportunity—than all of the Negroes on the continent of Africa and all of the two hundred million residents of Soviet Russia put together. But the Communists never allow such facts to interfere with their propaganda.

The Negro Communist is first and foremost the exponent of the *proletarian* revolution, for he realizes that this alone will guarantee not only freedom for the Negro but also emancipation of all toilers. [Italics in the original.]

Exactly the way they have been "emancipated," of course, in Soviet Russia.

The Communists fight for the right of the Black Belt territory to self-determination. This means not only that the Negro people shall no longer be oppressed but also shall come into their rightful position as the majority of the population in the Black Belt. It means equally the right of the Black Belt republic freely to determine its relations to the United States.

One cannot tell in advance under what circumstances the question of the right of self-determination for the Negro people in the Black Belt will arise for definite solution. There are two distinct possibilities.

First: The revolution in the plantation country might mature sooner than the proletarian revolution in the country as a whole. . . . Under these circumstances the Communists in the Black Belt would favor, and would do everything in their power to win the laboring people of the Black Belt to favor, complete independence from the capitalist-ruled republic of the North. . . .

Second: The proletarian revolution may overthrow capitalism and establish a Soviet Government for the country as a whole before the revolution comes to a head in the Black Belt. However it must be kept in mind that the two phases of the revolution will not develop separately. . . . One of the first steps of the central Soviet government will be to grant the right of self-determination to the Negro people in the Black Belt.

This would mean that the Negro people of the Black Belt will have the right to choose for themselves between federation with or separation from the United States as a whole. [Italics added.]

Whichever the Communists can bring about first, a total Soviet America, or a separate Soviet Negro Republic, and whether the Soviet Negro Republic chooses to remain entirely separate from or affiliated with the Soviet United States—when both have been established—

The actual extent of this new Republic . . . would be certain to include such cities as Richmond and Norfolk, Va., Columbia and Charleston, S. C., Atlanta, Augusta, Savannah and Macon, Georgia, Montgomery, Alabama, New Orleans and Shreveport, La., Little Rock, Arkansas, and Memphis, Tennessee.

The new government of this Soviet Negro Republic will arise in the form of local "Soviets" (that is, committees), to be formed while the revolution to establish "freedom and independence" is in process.

The Soviets which will arise in the old South will be somewhat as follows:

They will arise locally, here and there as the revolution starts, and spread as it develops further. Let us try to picture the composition of one of these Soviets, which will hold power in a certain locality. On this Soviet there will be representatives of the share-croppers, tenants and wage-workers of the plantations; then representatives, let us say, of the workers in a local sawmill or of a fertilizer plant, cotton gin, cotton-seed oil factory, or nearby textile mill; there might be one or two poor and small landowners. This Soviet will represent the interests of the workers from the mills and plantations and the poor farmers. It will embody the alliance between the workers and the poor farmers. It will be a dictatorship of these classes, using its power to defend the gains of the revolution and defeat all attempts of the former plantation masters and capitalists at counter-revolution.

As the gains of the revolution are consolidated these Soviet territories will unite to form the new Soviet Negro Republic.

And there, my friends, is both an explanation of the present turmoil and a preview of the future horror in our Dixie states. Identically the same formula of coercion by terror will be used, gradually and increasingly, to create some semblance of support for this "revolution" among the Negroes themselves as was used on the Moslems in Algeria—even though at least ninety-five percent of those southern Negroes will have wanted no part in any such "separatist" or "liberation" movement. Exactly the same diet of lies about what is really taking place in the South will be fed—and is already being fed—to the people of the rest of the United States as was given them for years about the Communist FLN activities in Algeria, so as to gain "bleeding heart" public opinion support of all kinds of fantastic governmental and diplomatic" moves on behalf of these noble seekers of "freedom and independence."

The same horror is deliberately planned for, and will be systematically developed in, the South as took place in Algeria and in dozens of other "colonial" areas of the world. A government in Washington dominated by Communist influences as completely as was the French government under de Gaulle and his predecessors will be doing everything it can and dares to help this "revolutionary movement" and these Communist purposes, always while pretending to be trying to prevent them—exactly as did de Gaulle. And despite all of the murders and vandalism which will be perpetrated on the white landowners and community leaders of every kind in the South, the Negroes themselves will be by far the greatest sufferers—both during the "revolution" and after it is successful—exactly as was the case for the Moslems in Algeria.

In due course, however, and at the proper point, the hedging and the pretense of change had to go even further. The time came for the Communists to bring about overt steps of national importance, such as the Supreme Court school-segregation decision of 1954 and the sending of federal troops into Arkansas by Eisenhower in 1958, which were designed to make the Negroes in the South feel that they were an oppressed colony and to create militant sympathy for the downtrodden colonial subjects throughout the rest of the nation. And the backlash from demands for a separate and "independent" Negro Soviet Republic were going to be too much of a load for their propaganda to carry. It was obviously wise for the Communists to wait until they had built up a suitable basis of turmoil in the South, and of confused liberal sentiment elsewhere in the nation, and until the Communist influence over our federal government was complete enough, before they could or should begin the FLN type of operation here. Otherwise, while the Negro Revolutionary Movement in the South itself might proceed all right by forced-draft propulsion according to formula, too much damage might be done to the broader "proletarian" national revolution, where great delicacy and deception were still needed.

So, while the Communists had reiterated their demand and support for a Negro Soviet Republic in 1951 in a mimeographed broadside of which they themselves claimed to have distributed a million copies, in 1959 it was felt that a sharp repudiation of this position was imperative. And thus, at the seventeenth national convention of the Communist Party, U.S.A., December 10 to 13, 1959, in the midst of gloating over the way Eisenhower's invitation to Khrushchev and Khrushchev's resulting state visit to our country had made it possible for the comrades to gain more influence in America, the convention passed a resolution discarding the party's historic position in advocacy of "self-determination" for Negroes.

This resolution was discussed by J. Edgar Hoover in a ten-page printed statement issued on January 26, 1960, by the Senate Internal Security Subcommittee. In this statement Mr. Hoover made this comment: "Time itself has shown that the [Communist] party is not interested in the welfare of the Negro, but only in using him as a tool to advance party interests." Then the Communist "theoretical and political magazine," *Political Affairs,* devoted an article of fifteen pages in its February 1960 issue to a new look "On the Negro Question in the United States," as a result of, and to explain, this ostensible about-face in Communist policy. This article insisted that the role of the Negroes in the total proletarian revolution in the United States had to be given primary consideration and emphasis. With regard to "this particular program" (namely, the demand for a black

belt Soviet Republic), *Political Affairs* said that "Life experience
and greater knowledge of the question have exposed its deficien-
cies and for this reason the 'self-determination' projection and
program for the solution of the Negro question in the United
States is hereby discarded."

But do not jump to any conclusions regarding this maneuver.
In our opinion it was a brilliant, temporary expedient, but only
that. Even in this very article in *Political Affairs*, the Communists laid the groundwork for future doubling back with such
italicized passages as the following: "*The question of Negro
freedom is the crucial domestic issue of the day and a factor of
international consequence.*" Even more important is the fact
that as recently as June of 1964 the executive committee of the
Communist Party, U.S.A., had a quiet new distribution made
of the Ford and Allen opus of 1934. Obviously this was a way of
emphasizing to the most important and most alert comrades that
this booklet still set forth the strategy and the tactics of the
future. And you might refresh your mind about the significance
of that gesture, as to what to expect from the NRM (Negro
Revolutionary Movement) in the years ahead, by going back
and reading our quotations above from the booklet in question—
especially those that we have italicized.

IV. THE GENERAL PROLETARIAN REVOLUTION

For convenience, let's refer to the total "proletarian" drive
for subversion of the United States as Revolution A, and to the
Negro Revolutionary Movement as Revolution N. As the Communists shift emphasis back and forth from one revolution to
the other, there is no basic change indicated—by the article in
Political Affairs or anywhere else—in the action program itself
with regard to the American Negro. The change is only in the
slogan under which that action program is to be carried forward.
To promote primarily Revolution N, the slogan had been, and
we feel sure in time will be again, "self-determination," or "national liberation," or the demand for a Negro Soviet Republic;

all of which, in Communist semantics, mean the same thing. To utilize agitation among Negroes, and propaganda about the oppression of Negroes, primarily in support of Revolution A, the slogan long has been "civil rights."

Since the early 1950's, or quite a while before the 1959 Communist convention repudiating "self-determination," the "civil rights" theme has been predominant. This may mean either that the Communists found the going for Revolution N tougher than they had expected, or the successful progress of Revolution A even more rapid than they had hoped. But in any event the Communist design, control, and uses of the "civil rights" movement remain equally clear. The program is as phony, in both premise and purpose, was was Mao Tse-tung's program under the slogan of "agrarian reform"—which supplied the Communist formula applicable to the present situation. The atrocities perpetrated by Mao Tse-tung on hundreds of thousands of Chinese peasants were just as cruel, whether he was trying to terrorize them into supporting "agrarian reform" or "self-determination." And the Communist propaganda in any case is just as deceptive, and just as effective in rallying the support of uninformed and gullible idealists outside the reach of these atrocities, whether it is based on "self-determination" or "agrarian reform" or "civil rights."

It does not really matter too much, therefore, which of the two concurrent "revolutions" the Communists are pushing harder at any given moment or how many times they reverse their lines—as they did with regard to being an enemy, then a bosom friend, and then again an enemy of Adolph Hitler, all in a period of a few months. It does not really matter whether or not, as we believe to be the case, the steps now taken under the slogan of "civil rights" can be made to fit into the progress of the NRM towards a black belt Soviet Republic. The important point is that the whole present "civil rights" drive, in both action and propaganda, consists of the most deceptive, fantastic, and incredible hypocrisy that has ever been put on display in American history.

The whole matrix of agitation, turmoil, rioting, and propaganda, which is currently designated by the phrase "civil rights," was never more accurately described than by the man who is now president of the United States. In a speech delivered in Austin, Texas, on May 22, 1948, Lyndon B. Johnson, obviously seeking to build up the southern backing which would eventually land him in the White House, made this statement:

The civil rights program, about which you have heard so much, is a farce and a sham—an effort to set up a police state in the guise of liberty. I am opposed to that program. I fought it in the Congress. It is the province of the state to run its own elections.

This analysis was eminently correct in every particular. It is still entirely correct. There has been no change since then, in either the so-called civil rights program itself or in the constitutionally guaranteed rights of the states to run their own elections. The change lies solely in Lyndon B. Johnson; or, more specifically, in the political course and pronouncements which now seem to him to serve best his present political purposes and ambitions.

As to the condition of the American Negro, which the Communists have been shouting that they were going to improve so much by applying on this continent the *successful* (!!) Soviet principles and procedures, it is well to ponder a statement written on January 24, 1948, by a famous New Orleans liberal, Edgar B. Stern. Mr. Stern saw and stated an important truth: "I would say without hesitation that the most humble Negro in America has greater security of life and person than any citizen of Russia or of its satellite countries." And Mr. Stern could also have added correctly that in 1948 the average American Negro had both a great deal more personal freedom, and a far higher material standard of living, than the average Russian, after a generation of all that glorious progress the Communists were claiming.

Since 1948 there have been some important changes with regard to the conditions of the American Negro.

(1) The educational opportunities of the Negroes in our

southern states have been tremendously improved. Some of these states have been spending as much as fifty percent of their total school budget on Negro schools, while deriving only fifteen percent of the money for that purpose from taxes paid by the Negro population. And this pattern was started long before, not because of, the 1954 Supreme Court school decision and the agitation which surrounded and followed that decision.

(2) The job opportunities for Negroes, and the progress of Negroes in the business and professional fields, have markedly increased. This has been despite a determined undercover effort by the Communists to prevent this trend. For, as Manning Johnson pointed out from his own knowledge and experience as a former high official of the party, the Communists did not want to improve the lot of the Negroes, but wanted just the opposite in order to maintain as much basis as possible for their agitation and propaganda.

(3) The "separate but equal" theory, which still applied to educational and other public facilities in about twenty percent of our states, had been rapidly gaining substance in the matter of equality, and losing rigidity in the matter of separateness. The net effect was, as pointed out a few years ago by America's leading Negro magazine, *Ebony*, that the United States had made and was making more headway in the honorable solution of a difficult racial problem than had ever been made by any other country.

But by 1954 the Communists were ready to start coming out into the open with activities that stimulated the Negro Revolutionary Movement, or that made "civil rights" agitation a substantial component of the total revolution, or did both. As to the real Communist purposes, instead of the pretended purposes of these activities; as to the small measure of local injustices which can be found, compared with the incredible turmoil and bitterness created over them throughout a whole nation; as to the role of the federal government in grossly violating the "civil rights" of all its citizens, when the guarantee of those rights is supposed to be what the "revolution" is all about; as to every aspect of the agitation and activities and propaganda, the whole "civil rights" movement is simply a gigantic fraud—or, as Lyndon Johnson put it in 1948, a sham and a farce. But it is a fraud which is leading, and has been designed to lead, through chaos and suffering and horror, through misunderstanding on the part of the deluded and paralysis of the will to resist on the part of the terrorized victims, to the police state of Communist tyranny.

There are those who believe that the simplest way to end the "movement," to prevent the ultimate tragedy, is for the people of the South—white and black—simply to concede at once every demand of the Communist-inspired agitators. But nothing could be further from the truth.

Chiang Kai-shek tried this solution in about 1946 with regard to the demands of the Chinese Reds under Mao Tse-tung. It was a fatal mistake. It is true that nobody could be more frustrated and disappointed, for a brief period, than would be the Communists behind the incitements to violence and bitterness in the South, if their front men were suddenly given every single thing they are rioting and shouting for with so much clamor. Just as Mao was almost thrown off *his* stride of terror when this unexpected tragedy happened to him in China. But the respite here, as it was there, would be too short-lived. In such cases the Communists immediately think up even more impractical and preposterous "reforms"—to be enforced immediately by law and guns, instead of gradually by good will and education— which new "reforms" they push with even more ruthlessness and violence while they are flush with their visible success as to earlier demands.

We have had many examples of how far afield from justice or common sense the Communists will go to proclaim oppression where none exists and to demand "reforms" where none are needed. Boston offers an excellent illustration. As far back as forty-six years ago when this writer first came to Massachusetts, every single privilege and right of our Negro citizens for which these marches in the South are presently being organized were already commonplace. I sat beside a Negro in one class at Harvard Law School. I frequently found a Negro student sitting beside me at lunch. There were no handicaps of any kind on Negro voting; no segregated schools; no segregated public facilities; and no legal or formal segregation of any kind. Today even the informal integration—social, political, and economic—has been carried so much further that a Negro politician, who is married to a white woman, was elected and is at present serving as attorney general of the commonwealth. You certainly would not think the "civil rights" agitators could find anything to complain about in Boston.

But does that stop them from demanding "reforms" or threatening riots to enforce such demands? Not at all. Where no reasons for complaint exist, such reasons have to be invented. In Boston, the chief of these inventions has been the complaint that the schools are racially imbalanced; and strident demands are made that pupils be hauled daily by buses to and from schools in parts of the city distant from their homes, instead of going to the schools built to serve their neighborhoods—so as to remedy this "racial imbalance." And when agitators incite or coerce Negroes in Boston to parade and picket and clamor for "freedom," the whole sham and farce—as Lyndon Johnson called it —is both nefarious and idiotic, but no more so than the march from Selma to Montgomery led by Martin Luther King. In neither case are the real instigators of these parades or marches interested at all in the ostensible objectives, but only in the by-products along the route of "reform."

As to handicaps to Negro voting in a few southern states, or other less specific injustices in many states, there undoubtedly still remain some examples. These should be corrected. But they could be and were being corrected without creating any mountains to bring forth a mouse. To tear a whole great nation to pieces, and to try to plunge a large part of it into civil war, over the few such injustices as do exist, is on a par with sinking a mighty ship in order to get a rat out of the scupper. Except in this case the Communists behind the operation do not even care about getting rid of the rat. Sinking the ship is their real purpose all the way.

V. AND THE ANSWER TO BOTH

The only way to solve the problem at hand and prevent the horror ahead is, in our opinion, the only way to deal with all other aspects of the Communist conspiracy as a whole. And that is, simply to bring about enough understanding on the part of enough people of what the Communists are trying to do, and how they are trying to do it, and how much progress they have already made. It still takes the Communists quite a while to build up in the public mind an acceptance as truth of their falsehoods, deceptions, and propaganda. But they must have this acceptance in order to forestall the opposition which they would otherwise meet as Communist terror becomes more extensive and pro-Communist political moves more brazen.

The deliberate manufacture of falsehoods and false impressions about what is actually taking place in the South is now reaching the same level that was maintained by Communist propaganda about Algeria for years. And none of these falsehoods and distortions could be accepted or believed by even the most gullible and idealistic citizens of other states, if enough people in those states realized that the whole show was being stage-managed by Communists behind the scenes. And especially if these good people realized that the tactics used are all exactly in accordance with plans the Communists have been laying out in writing for their own agents ever since the 1920's, and which they have repeatedly utilized without any significant changes in other areas all over the world.

The truth is that the infamous picture of a dog attacking a Negro, while the dog was held in leash by a Birmingham police officer, was so carefully rehearsed until the "civil rights" agitators got exactly the picture they wanted, that the leg of the Negro victim's trousers had even been cut with a razor in advance so that it would fall apart more readily at the first touch by the dog. Yet this picture was shown on the front pages of newspapers all over the United States—most of which did not know it was a contrived phony—and became an extremely important part of the Communist propaganda about "civil rights."

Actually, it is not even necessary to cite specific instances of such mischievous misreporting or fabrication, if the American people will only stop to think, and use the common sense God has given them. No matter what state you are in, for instance, ask yourself how you would like to have a huge flood of trouble-making outsiders from all over the country shipped into your state for the specific purpose of breaking its laws—all under the pretense of correcting some fault of your state, while crime and immorality and injustice are rampant in their own. When you add to that situation the fact that a large number of the trouble-making leaders on the forefront of this invasion are known to be Communists, fellow travelers, or Communist fronters, you certainly would not be happy about a similar development around you. And you have no more reason to be happy about it, or to give these actions your moral support—even through tacit lack of protest—than do the good people to whom it is actually happening in the states of Alabama and Mississippi.

As to the pro-Communist personnel among these invaders, we call your attention to a recent speech by Senator Eastland on the floor of the Senate which was printed in the *Congressional Record* for February 3, 1965. He needed many pages of fine print to give the detailed record and documentation on the Communist affiliations of just the leading lawyers in the group organized in New York and California to go to Mississippi and obtain hundreds of depositions in an effort to unseat the five congressmen now serving in our House of Representatives from that state. The same would be true with regard to similar groups of invaders who have gone to Alabama and Mississippi for parallel purposes in connection with the whole synthetic turmoil which has been created there.

We contend that if enough people come to know these facts, and to understand the Communist influences at work in the total picture, the whole "civil rights" agitation and Negro Revolutionary Movement will all collapse as did the defense of Alger Hiss when the truth at long last became obvious to the court and the jury. And we hope that every patriotic reader will help us, as far as he is able, to reach other readers with this truth. The stakes in this struggle of truth against falsehood are as high as they have ever been in history.

Wake up yourself, and wake up your friends and neighbors and associates to the part being played by the federal government, by the National Council of Churches, and by much of the press—although in general more unwittingly—in advancing Communist purposes, in demoralizing opposition to Communism, and in tearing to pieces the safeguards and framework of our Constitution. And since a single illustrative example frequently brings the beginning of understanding better than a general survey, you might want to use Martin Luther King as an introductory exhibit.

For few private citizens have wielded more influence in shaping the domestic policies of our federal government than has King, and few have deserved this power and prestige less. Even Joseph Alsop says that King "has accepted and is almost certainly still accepting Communist collaboration and even Communist advice." And this was putting the matter very mildly indeed.

For an illustration, King employed one Jack O'Dell as a top-level aide from 1960 to 1963, even though O'Dell was a known member of the National Committee of the Communist Party, U.S.A., and was officially so listed on their letterhead of November 1961. For another, Martin Luther King himself attended the Highlander Folk School, in Monteagle, Tennessee, over Labor Day weekend in 1957. The record is clear that this institution was a "Communist training school." That same school now operates as the Highlander Center, in Knoxville, Tennessee; and as recently as May 1963 the letterhead of Highlander Center listed Martin Luther King as one of its official sponsors.

Among other close associates of King are James Dombrowski,

and Carl and Anne Braden, all three identified under oath as Communists; and Bayard Rustin, who joined the Young Communist League in 1936, and whose pro-Communist activities and criminal career are all a matter of record. Rustin served as King's secretary for five years, and accompanied King to Norway in December 1964, when King was given the Nobel Peace Prize. A full listing and documentation of King's connection with Communists would take many pages. And in the face of this record King simply revealed his own character by his recent claim that "there are as many Communists in the freedom movement as there are Eskimos in Florida." This brazen statement itself follows the Communist technique: "L'audace, toujours l'audace!"

The tremendous "honors" heaped upon King reveal two things: (1) How far King has gone in establishing himself as the favorite of the Communists, or as the Ben Bella of the Negro Revolutionary Movement; and (2) how far Communist influences have gone in subverting great prize committees and universities to the service of Communist propaganda and purposes. The fact that Yale University once gave Martin Luther King an honorary degree does not make King any less the "notorious liar" which J. Edgar Hoover called him, nor any less of a troublemaker pushing pro-Communist programs than his record proves him to be. It merely shows the utterly disgraceful level to which Yale University—along with many other institutions of higher *learning*—has been brought by the influences which now control it. As for the real significance of the Nobel Peace Prize, we published nearly ten years ago the plain fact that even then, for all practical purposes, the Nobel Prize committees had become simply propaganda agencies of the Soviet government.

A more detailed study of "the life and lies" of Martin Luther King from plenty of materials which are available will convince any reasonable American that this man is not working for, *but against*, the real welfare and best interests of either the Negroes in the United States, or of the United States as a whole. And the same thing is true of many of the other leaders in the "two revolutions at once" which now beset our nation.

Finally, let us repeat once again: The fundamentally decent American mind simply refuses to recognize the nature of the beasts with whom we are now engaged in the most completely all-out struggle that the human race has ever known. But it had better be recognizing these realities soon, or all decency will be deliberately wiped off the face of our planet. For if and when the United States goes the way of Czechoslovakia and China and Cuba and the Congo, not only will our own freedom, our lives, and our country be lost, but our whole civilization will be destroyed.

Index

Photo by Fabian Bac